CHRIST IS
VICTOR

AF579794

CHRIST IS VICTOR

edited by
W. Glyn
Evans

Judson Press ® Valley Forge

CHRIST IS VICTOR

Library of Congress Cataloging in Publication Data
Main entry under title:

Christ is victor.

1. Jesus Christ—Crucifixion—Sermons. 2. Jesus Christ—Resurrection—Sermons. I. Evans, William Glynn. II. Title.
BT268.C46 232.9'63 77-79774
ISBN 0-8170-0756-3

Printed in the U.S.A. 

ACKNOWLEDGMENTS

The author gratefully acknowledges permission to reprint the messages of this book from the following publishers as listed below:

"On the Day of the Crucifixion" by Leonid N. Andreev. © Copyright *Christianity Today* 1957. Reprinted by permission.

"The Cross—History or Experience?" by William Ward Ayer. From *Clothed Skeletons* (Grand Rapids, Mich.: Zondervan Publishing House, 1946). Used by permission.

"Death Abolished!" by J. Sidlow Baxter. Reprinted by permission, from the April issue of *Moody Monthly,* copyright 1963, Moody Bible Institute of Chicago.

"The Basic Issue" by Donald Bloesch. From *Decision,* © 1975 by the Billy Graham Evangelistic Association, Minneapolis, Minnesota.

"Behind the Bronze Doors of Calvary" by James M. Boice. Reprinted by permission of *Eternity* magazine, copyright 1969, The Evangelical Foundation, 1716 Spruce St., Philadelphia, PA 19103.

"He Could Have Saved Himself" by Bob W. Brown. Reprinted by permission of *Eternity* magazine, copyright 1968, The Evangelical Foundation, 1716 Spruce St., Philadelphia, PA 19103.

"Depersonalization and Resurrection Faith" by Myron R. Chartier. © Copyright *Christianity Today* 1968. Reprinted by permission.

"The Suffering Savior" by Edmund P. Clowney. From *Decision,* © 1976 by the Billy Graham Evangelistic Association, Minneapolis, Minnesota.

"The Literal Resurrection of Christ" by W. A. Criswell. From *Why I Preach the Bible Is Literally True* (Nashville: Broadman Press, 1969). Used by permission.

"The Road to Galilee" by W. Glyn Evans. Reprinted by permission, from the June issue of *Moody Monthly,* copyright 1961, Moody Bible Institute of Chicago.

"We Celebrate Jesus As Lord of All" by Gerhard E. Frost. © Copyright *Christianity Today* 1966. Reprinted by permission.

"The Living Christ" by Frank E. Gaebelein. © Copyright *Christianity Today* 1975. Reprinted by permission.

"We Walk Backward into the Future" by Stuart P. Garver. Reprinted from *Christian Heritage,* March, 1975, Hackensack, New Jersey. Used by permission.

"Tell Everyone It Is True" by Billy Graham. From *Decision,* © 1974 by the Billy Graham Evangelistic Association, Minneapolis, Minnesota.

"Easter Christians" by Oswald C. J. Hoffmann. Reprinted from *Christian Herald,* April, 1960, Chappaqua, New York. Used by permission.

"I, Pilate" by Harold F. Leestma. From *Decision,* © 1972 by the Billy Graham Evangelistic Association, Minneapolis, Minnesota.

"Easter's Prelude" by Douglas N. Moffat. Reprinted from *Canadian Baptist,* March, 1974, Toronto, Ontario. Used by permission.

"Unsentimental Jesus" by Joel Nederhood. Reprinted by permission from *His,* student magazine of Inter-Varsity Christian Fellowship, © 1973.

"Understanding Calvary" by Harold John Ockenga. © Copyright *Christianity Today* 1957. Reprinted by permission.

"The Inevitable Cross" by David H. C. Read. From *I Am Persuaded* (Edinburgh: T. & T. Clark, 1961). Used by permission.

"Backwards or Forwards?" by Samuel M. Shoemaker © Copyright *Christianity Today* 1959. Reprinted by permission.

"The Hurting and Healing Gaze of God" by K. M. Swenson. Reprinted from *New Pulpit Digest,* March, 1971, Keuka Park, New York. Used by permission.

"The Paradox of the Cross" by Rodrigo D. Tano. Reprinted from *Alliance Witness,* January, 1976, Nyack, New York. Used by permission.

CONTENTS

Introduction 9

ON THE DAY OF THE CRUCIFIXION 11
Leonid N. Andreev

THE CROSS—HISTORY OR EXPERIENCE? 15
William Ward Ayer

DEATH ABOLISHED! 21
J. Sidlow Baxter

THE BASIC ISSUE 27
Donald Bloesch

BEHIND THE BRONZE DOORS OF CALVARY 31
James M. Boice

HE COULD HAVE SAVED HIMSELF 35
Bob W. Brown

DEPERSONALIZATION AND RESURRECTION FAITH 41
Myron R. Chartier

THE SUFFERING SAVIOR 47
Edmund P. Clowney

THE LITERAL RESURRECTION OF CHRIST 51
W. A. Criswell

THE ROAD TO GALILEE 57
W. Glyn Evans

WE CELEBRATE JESUS AS LORD OF ALL 63
Gerhard E. Frost

THE LIVING CHRIST 67
Frank E. Gaebelein

WE WALK BACKWARD INTO THE FUTURE 71
Stuart P. Garver

TELL EVERYONE IT IS TRUE 77
Billy Graham

EASTER CHRISTIANS 81
Oswald C. J. Hoffmann

I, PILATE 85
Harold F. Leestma

EASTER'S PRELUDE 91
Douglas N. Moffat

UNSENTIMENTAL JESUS 97
Joel Nederhood

UNDERSTANDING CALVARY 103
Harold John Ockenga

THE INEVITABLE CROSS 109
David H. C. Read

BACKWARDS OR FORWARDS? 115
Samuel M. Shoemaker

THE HURTING AND HEALING GAZE OF GOD 121
K. M. Swenson

THE PARADOX OF THE CROSS 125
Rodrigo D. Tano

INTRODUCTION

The responses of friends and well-wishers to an earlier editorial work (*He Has Come: Messages Proclaiming the Birth of Christ,* Broadman Press, 1975) have encouraged me to try the same editorial attempt on another facet of our Lord's earthly ministry—his death and resurrection. As in my earlier work, I scoured as many locations as possible for meaningful messages on Christ's sufferings and eventual triumph in resurrection. I especially sought messages which strongly emphasized the hope which Christ imparts to us because he came back from the grave victoriously and that his victory is meaningful to us *now*. This is the theme which I have tried to highlight in the selections found in this work.

Because of this hopeful aspect, I feel these messages will benefit ministers by strengthening their preaching in the Lenten and Easter seasons. And if I may judge from the response to my volume of Christmas sermons, lay people will also benefit from fresh insights into the personal meaning of Christ's death and resurrection.

Again I am indebted—as any compiler must be—to my friends and acquaintances who have encouraged me in this work and to librarians who have assisted me in securing materials. A special word of thanks should go to Mary Alexander and Ruth Crane, my office assistants, who worked so loyally on the details of the manuscript.

With confidence in the reality of the risen Christ I send this out as a token of my comradeship with every believer and especially with those who stand, as I stand, proclaiming triumphantly, "Christ is Victor!"

ON THE DAY OF THE CRUCIFIXION

LEONID N. ANDREEV

On that day when Jesus Christ was crucified between robbers on Golgotha—on that day from early morning Ben-Tovit, a tradesman of Jerusalem, suffered from an unendurable toothache. His toothache had commenced on the day before, toward evening. At first his right jaw started to pain him and one tooth seemed to have risen somewhat; and when his tongue touched the tooth, he felt a painful sensation. After supper, however, his toothache passed, and Ben-Tovit had forgotten all about it. He had made a profitable deal on that day. He had bartered an old donkey for a young, strong one; so he was very cheerful and paid no heed to any ominous signs.

And he slept very soundly. But just before daybreak something began to disturb him, as if someone were calling him on a very important matter, and when Ben-Tovit awoke angrily, his teeth were aching, aching openly and maliciously, causing him an acute, drilling pain. And he could no longer understand whether it was only the same tooth that had ached on the previous day, or whether others had joined that tooth; Ben-Tovit's entire mouth and his head were filled with terrible sensations of pain, as though he had been forced to chew

Leonid N. Andreev was a Russian writer who bitterly opposed the Bolshevists when they seized power in 1917. As a result of his opposition, he was forced to leave his native land and he became a refugee, finally locating in Finland where he later died in poor and distressed circumstances. This story is a reflection of his deep Christian devotion and zeal.

thousands of sharp, red-hot nails. He took some water into his mouth from an earthen jug—for a minute the acuteness of the pain subsided, his teeth twitched and swayed like a wave, and this sensation was even pleasant as compared with the other.

Ben-Tovit lay down again, recalled his new donkey, and thought how happy he would have been if not for his toothache, and he wanted to fall asleep. But the water was warm, and five minutes later his toothache began to rage more severely than ever. Ben-Tovit sat up in his bed and swayed back and forth like a pendulum. His face became wrinkled and seemed to have shrunk, and a drop of cold perspiration was hanging on his nose, which had turned pale from his sufferings. Thus, swaying back and forth and groaning for pain, he met the first rays of the sun, which were destined to see Golgotha and the three crosses and grow dim from horror and sorrow.

Ben-Tovit was a good and kind man who hated any injustice; but when his wife awoke, he said many unpleasant things to her, opening his mouth with difficulty, and he complained that he was left alone, like a jackal, to groan and writhe for pain. His wife met the undeserved reproaches patiently, for she knew that they came not from an angry heart; and she brought him numerous good remedies: rats' litter to be applied to his cheek, some strong liquid in which a scorpion was preserved, and a real chip of the tablets that Moses had broken. He began to feel a little better from the rats' litter, but not for long, also from the liquid and the stone, but the pain returned each time with renewed intensity.

During the moments of rest Ben-Tovit consoled himself with the thought of the little donkey, and he dreamed of him; and when he felt worse, he moaned, scolded his wife, and threatened to dash his head against a rock if the pain should not subside. He kept pacing back and forth on the flat roof of his house from one corner to the other, feeling ashamed to come close to the side facing the street, for his head was tied around with a kerchief, like that of a woman. Several times children came running to him and told him hastily about Jesus of Nazareth. Ben-Tovit paused, listened to them for a while, his face wrinkled, but then he stamped his foot angrily and chased them away. He was a kind man and he loved children, but now he was angry at them for bothering him with trifles.

It was disagreeable to him that a large crowd had gathered in the street and on the neighboring roofs, doing nothing and looking curiously at Ben-Tovit, with his head tied around with a kerchief like a woman. He was about to go down when his wife said to him: "Look, they are leading robbers there. Perhaps that will divert you."

"Let me alone. Don't you see how I am suffering?" Ben-Tovit answered angrily.

But there was a vague promise in his wife's words that there might be a relief for his toothache; so he walked over to the parapet unwillingly. Bending his head on one side, closing one eye, and supporting his cheek with his hand, he assumed a squeamish, weeping expression, and he looked toward the street.

On the narrow street going uphill, an enormous crowd was moving forward in disorder, covered with dust and shouting uninterruptedly. In the middle of the crowd walked the criminals, bending down under the weight of their crosses, and over them the scourges of the Roman soldiers were wriggling about like black snakes. One of the men, he of the long, light hair, in a torn, blood-stained cloak, stumbled over a stone which was thrown under his feet, and he fell. The shouting grew louder, and the crowd, like colored seawater, closed in about the man on the ground. Ben-Tovit suddenly shuddered for pain; he felt as though someone had pierced a red-hot needle into his tooth and turned it there; he groaned and walked away from the parapet, angry and squeamishly indifferent.

"How they are shouting!" he said enviously, picturing to himself their wide-open mouths with strong, healthy teeth and how he himself would have shouted if he had been well. This intensified his toothache, and he shook his muffled head frequently and roared, "Moo-Moo . . ."

"They say that he restored sight to the blind," said his wife, who remained standing at the parapet, and she threw down a little cobblestone near the place where Jesus, lifted by the whips, was moving again slowly.

"Of course, of course! He should have cured my toothache," replied Ben-Tovit ironically, and he added bitterly with irritation: "What dust they have kicked up! Like a herd of cattle! They should all be driven away with a stick! Take me down, Sarah!"

The wife proved to be right. The spectacle had diverted Ben-Tovit slightly—perhaps it was the rats' litter that had helped after all—and he later succeeded in falling asleep. When he awoke, his toothache had passed almost entirely, and only a little inflammation had formed over his right jaw. His wife told him that it was not noticeable at all, but Ben-Tovit smiled cunningly; he knew how kindhearted his wife was and how fond she was of telling him pleasant things.

Samuel the tanner, a neighbor of Ben-Tovit's, came in, and Ben-Tovit led him to see the new little donkey and listened proudly to the warm praises for himself and his animal.

Then, at the request of the curious Sarah, the three went to Golgotha to see the people who had been crucified. On the way Ben-Tovit told Samuel in detail how he had felt a pain in his right jaw on the day before and how he awoke at night with a terrible toothache. To illustrate it, he made a martyr's face, closing his eyes, shaking his head, and groaning while the gray-bearded Samuel nodded his head compassionately and said, "Oh, how painful it must have been!"

Ben-Tovit was pleased with Samuel's attitude and he repeated the story to him, then went back to the past when his first tooth was spoiled on the left side. Thus, absorbed in a lively conversation, they reached Golgotha. The sun, which was destined to shine upon the world on that terrible day, had already set beyond the distant hills; and in the west a narrow, purple-red strip was burning, like a stain of blood. The crosses stood out darkly but vaguely against this background, and at the foot of the middle cross, white kneeling figures were seen indistinctly.

The crowd had long ago dispersed; it was growing chilly, and after a glance at the crucified men, Ben-Tovit took Samuel by the arm and carefully turned him in the direction of his house. He felt that he was particularly eloquent just then, and he was eager to finish the story of his toothache. Thus they walked, and Ben-Tovit made a martyr's face, shook his head and groaned skillfully, while Samuel nodded compassionately and uttered exclamations from time to time; and from the deep, narrow defiles, out of the distant, burning plains rose the black night. It seemed as though the night wished to hide from the view of heaven the great crime of the earth.

THE CROSS—HISTORY OR EXPERIENCE?

WILLIAM WARD AYER

One trouble with the world, the real reason it is in serious straits, is that it has left the cross out of its thinking and planning.

Go into the halls of Congress, where men wrangle about the conditions of the present and pass laws with the hope of bringing improvement to the future, and you will discover that all of the planning is on a social basis, with no room for the cross's redemptive ministry. Look in on the latest world assembly—"the new parliament of man" looking toward "the federation of the world": the United Nations Assembly—and you will hear the most boastful talking of modern times. There also you will see men struggling with gigantic and insurmountable problems of international intrigue, commercial competition, national aggrandizement: procedure which always leads to war, and war in this atomic age means the annihilation of our civilization.

Born in New Brunswick, Canada, **William Ward Ayer** eventually moved to Boston where, under the ministry of Billy Sunday, he found Christ. He received his education from Moody Bible Institute, Lincoln College, and Northern Baptist Seminary. He served churches in Illinois and Indiana before becoming pastor of Philpott Tabernacle, Hamilton, Ontario, in 1932. From 1936 to 1949 he had a fruitful ministry as pastor of Calvary Baptist Church, New York City. His success as radio preacher earned him the title "Third Citizen of New York," in a poll conducted by WOR in 1947. Several books have come from his pen, including *Seven Saved Sinners, Clothed Skeletons,* and others. He continues a busy ministry from St. Petersburg, Florida, as editor of *Marching Truth Magazine.*

Undoubtedly earnest people are there—men who desire to set up a world organization which will protect the peoples of the nations from the periodic insanity of war—but you will listen in vain for any word that tells of a knowledge of the redemptive work of God in the world through the cross of Jesus Christ.

Ask them, "What place do you give the cross?" and their answers will be pathetic. They will smile blandly and reply, "The cross? Oh, yes, a delightful religious symbol." Some a little more learned will venture, "The cross? . . . yes, a universal principle, a high ideal. The race hasn't attained to that ideal as yet; and until it does, we must work on lower levels." "The cross?" Others will comment, "It is two thousand years too old; it does not belong in the twentieth century. We must have something more modern."

Yes, that's the trouble with the world: the cross is left out of its thinking and planning, although the cross is basic in world redemption. Here's the problem: God planted the cross on Calvary's hill to save the world from the very calamities which now blight us, but men have ignored the cross—its message and its power—and are endeavoring, as God says in Romans, "to establish their own righteousness, having rejected the righteousness of God" (see Romans 10:3*b*). Yet there is one hopeful thing about all this: the forces of evil, operative through evil men and nations, cannot conquer this world while the cross stands upon Calvary's hill!

We are told that the great Napoleon after conquering almost the whole of Europe put his finger on a red spot on the map indicating the British Isles and remarked, "Were it not for that red spot, I would conquer the world." Hitler realized the same thing apparently; he, too, failed because Britain was not defeated. This is a figure and a symbol of God's great red spot on the map of the world: the red spot of Calvary. Sin and Satan would soon conquer all but for the cross, which stands fast.

Now while the nations in their efforts for peace ignore the cross of Christ, they fail to realize that no peace can be had apart from the cross. They have not learned that it was upon the cross that peace was made—peace between God and man, peace between man and man—for the Lord Jesus made peace by the blood of his cross. Despite their ignorance God is using the cross as the instrument of his eternal purposes in the world.

There is deep tragedy here, for men will not learn God's truth. One could wish for someone like Elijah of old to be raised up with courage enough to walk into the arrogant and muddled sessions of the United Nations with the blazing eye, glowing face, and pointing finger of the old prophet who faced Ahab and his courtiers—someone brave enough to tell them in stentorian tones of the futility of their struggles while Jesus Christ is ignored.

It is sad to remember that if the churches of Christ throughout the world had been faithful in preaching the gospel, these men sitting in the halls of Congress and at the tables of the UN sessions would know the truth. The church has failed miserably, however, in teaching people God's purposes in the world; so perhaps she has little right to condemn the world's ignorance. Too often the church herself has been faithless to the cross, its meaning and its power.

What is the cross to us? This is our study.

First, think of the cross historical. Primarily the cross is not sentiment, though we have wreathed a great many sentimental bouquets round about it. Fundamentally the cross is history. Christ died. That's a great historical fact, as truly history as that Julius Caesar was assassinated or that Lincoln died from a murderous bullet. The death of Christ is a fact in time, an historical event. You will still find some fools who deny that he ever existed; to them the cross is a fable. The life and death of Christ are, however, well-attested facts.

While the cross of Christ is an historical fact, in order to have power, it must be much more than history. Historical events are largely devoid of moral or spiritual power. As a matter of fact, multitudes say of the death of Christ: "Why make so much fuss over a man who died on a cross two thousand years ago? Martyrs are nothing new in the world. Noble men have given their lives to causes; rivers of blood have run. Jesus is only one of many; in fact, he died in a period of martyrdom. Historians say that in the forty years between Pilate and Titus thirty thousand Jews were crucified by the Romans. Jesus was only one of these. Why should we be so concerned with this one Jew and his unhappy demise?"

If the cross is history alone, we need not be wrought up over the matter; but if we look closely at that cross, noting the nature of the One who died there, we realize immediately that the cross could not be a merely historical event. We must look at the Man and think of his wisdom and his power over nature, disease, death, the elements; mark his humility and his supreme dignity. Even the enemies of this Man testified to his perfection: Pilate saying, "I find no fault in him"; Judas declaring in remorse, "I have betrayed innocent blood"; and the centurion being forced to proclaim that Jesus was the Son of God.

Then look at the cross theological. Now we begin to see its meaning. We declare not only that Christ died but also that Christ died for our sins; there was meaning, divine meaning, to his death. History declares that a man named Jesus lived in time and died upon a Roman cross. Theology says that God in human form inserted himself in the person of Jesus at a specific time in human history for the definite purpose of human redemption and that the cross of Calvary was the focal point of that redemptive work of the Son of God, whose human name was Jesus.

The Gospels tell the historic facts of the death of Christ; the Epistles are filled with declarations of the meaning of it. Such passages as

> "He made him to be sin for us, who knew no sin; that we might be made the righteousness of God in him" (2 Corinthians 5:21, KJV); "God was in Christ, reconciling the world unto himself, not imputing their trespasses unto them . . ." (2 Corinthians 5:19, KJV)

and scores of others give theological meaning to an historical event.

We need a correct theology, but theology cannot save. The present-day blight of Christianity is manifested in this: thousands have the doctrine but know little of the life.

Then there is the cross experiential. We have noted that "Christ died" is history, that "Christ died for our sins" is theology; but Paul goes further when he says, "[He] loved me and gave himself for me" (Galatians 2:20). This is experience; and unless we come to this place in our appreciation of the cross, its major power is lost to us.

It is surprising how few people recognize the personal element in the cross. Until we've seen the fact that Jesus died for each one of us individually, we've never really seen Calvary. It means little in the mass. We read almost with indifference of a hundred thousand people killed in concentration camps; we are more moved by the story of five people killed in an accident. A capable author can stir us to our depths in telling of the death of one man. In the same manner the purpose of the death of Christ must be individualized before we truly appreciate it. We quote glibly, "God so loved the world, that he gave his only begotten Son" (John 3:16); that generalizes the message and generalizations are usually ineffective. Christ's death must be particularized.

When I was a pastor in Indiana, a young man from a Christian home came to talk to me about his spiritual problem.

"Pastor," he began, "I've always thought I was a Christian. My mother taught me to believe everything that you've been preaching, but some of the things you've been saying make me wonder whether I am really a child of God or not."

I questioned him concerning the fundamentals of the faith, and he said, "Of course I believe those things."

I said, "Do you believe that Jesus died for your sins?"

He replied, "Of course, I have always believed that."

He was indeed a problem. I probed a little deeper.

"Charlie," I said, "tell me: if you were the only person that ever lived and you found yourself in the condition you are now in, do you believe that Jesus would have had to come and die for you?"

He replied immediately, "Why, of course not! He died for the whole world and I suppose in that sense he died for me, but I don't think he died for me personally."

"Well, Charlie," I said, "if you really want to know that you're a child of God, you must realize that Jesus Christ bore your sins in his own body on the tree just as if you were the only person that had ever lived." And I believe that we cannot appreciate or appropriate the cross until we see it in that way.

It is not an unpleasant thought that Jesus died for everybody. If you are willing, the Holy Spirit will show you that Jesus Christ came to die for you personally—you who were a lost sinner, a miserable worm of an individual, lost and undone. Realize that the Lord Jesus Christ took your place in judgment as definitely and specifically as though you were the only person in all the universe, and you'll feel the truth of the lines

My sins gave sharpness to the nails
And pointed every thorn.

One day a servant knocked at the door of Martin Luther's study and receiving no response burst into his presence to find the great reformer prostrated before a crucifix. Obviously the Spirit of God had shown this leader the personal nature of Calvary, for he was weeping and crying, "The cross, the cross; for me, for me!"

Dr. Alexander Whyte tells the story of a man who dreamed that he saw Jesus tied to a whipping post while a soldier scourged him. He saw the whip in the soldier's hand, its thick lashes studded here and there with bits of lead which were intended to cut into the flesh. As he brought the whip down on the bare shoulders of Jesus, the dreamer shuddered to see the welts and bloodstains it left behind. When the soldier raised his arm to strike again, the dreamer rushed forward intending to stop him; as he did so, the soldier turned around and the dreamer recognized himself!

We often think how cruel those men must have been who scourged and crucified the Lord Jesus, but in a spiritual sense it was not alone the Jews and Romans who crucified the Son of God; we were all there at Calvary; we all had a part in the transaction.

Oh, that we might be able to say with the apostle: "God forbid that I should glory, save in the cross of our Lord Jesus Christ, by whom the world is crucified unto me, and I unto the world" (Galatians 6:14, KJV).

DEATH ABOLISHED!

J. SIDLOW BAXTER

Some years ago news was spread around that the bones of Buddha had been discovered. When the supposed bones were brought to India's most sacred city, multitudes of devotees lined the streets to pay homage. A Christian missionary, watching them as they superstitiously prostrated themselves, remarked to a friend, "If they could find one bone of Jesus Christ, Christianity would fall to pieces."

That comment is true: the bodily resurrection of Jesus is the prime apologetic of our Christian faith. This planet of ours will always bear the crimson seal of Calvary, where God incarnate shed his blood to redeem our fallen race; but there is no grave anywhere in the earth's crust which holds that crucified body!

Yes, Jesus rose and Jesus lives; and what titanic meaning that has for the future of our human race! In a world blinded by Satan, and blighted by sin, and blasted by war; amid the gloomy problems which beset the unfolding future, the one great fact which gives solid

J. Sidlow Baxter was born in Sydney, Australia, and received his education at Spurgeon's College, London. He held pastorates in Northampton and Sunderland, England, and Edinburgh, Scotland. Since 1955 he has engaged in a worldwide Bible teaching ministry. He holds the Doctor of Divinity degree from Central Baptist Seminary, Toronto. A talented writer, Baxter has written *Explore the Book, Mark These Men, Our High Calling,* and many other books. He now resides in Santa Barbara, California.

comfort, hope, and promise is that nineteen hundred and some years ago God raised up the crucified Jesus from the grave.

That empty tomb means *Diabolos* vanquished and Christ victorious. It means that in the next chapter of human history God's kingdom will come and that his will shall be done on earth as it is done in heaven.

The biggest problem of the natural man during this present age is the silence of God. "Why does not God speak?" he asks. "Let God speak, so that we may hear him and know that he really is."

The resurrection of Christ proclaims that God *has* spoken already and that the God who spoke yesterday will speak again in a soon-coming morrow. As truly as Jesus rose, he will come to this earth again. His resurrection tolls the knell on evil's dark kingdom and rings the glad bell of God-given hope for our travailing earth.

Since the splitting of the atom, the rise of Communist totalitarianism, and the resuscitation of Israel as a self-governing nation, the present age, I believe, is rushing on with accentuated momentum to the world's Friday night. The morning of the seventh-day, thousand-year millennial sabbath is soon to break upon our war-weary world, when the Christ of the Easter morn shall become the Christ of the Davidic throne; when men shall beat their swords to ploughshares and their spears to pruning hooks, and the earth shall learn war no more.

With such thoughts stirring our minds afresh, let us look again at these vivid words of the apostle Paul: "Our Saviour Christ Jesus . . . *abolished death*" (2 Timothy 1:10, KJV, italics added). What does that mean? Paul does not say merely that Jesus rose from the grave. To say that he rose states only the fact; but to say that he "abolished death" utters one of the profound *meanings* of that fact. Note carefully that the statement is in the past tense: "He abolished death." The reference is not to something which he is yet going to do in a climactic future, but to something which he did within the ranks of historical humanity over nineteen hundred years ago.

Yet that raises an urgent question: If he abolished death at that time, why does death still continue to be the monster-slayer of mankind? Are we not all travelers to the grave? Is not the pessimistic old dirge still true: "The newborn infant's earliest breath is life's first prophecy of death"? In what sense, then, did our Lord "abolish death"?

In the first place, he abolished death by breaking its power over *himself.* First he underwent it. Then he overcame it. He need not have died, even when they spiked him to the cross. One slight exertion of his inherent divine power, and he could have descended in swift destruction upon his crucifiers. One word of command from him, and twelve legions of angels would have swooped down to annihilate the wicked schemers who had contrived his murder. But he allowed himself to expire on the cross. He allowed his body to become a corpse and to be buried. He allowed himself in disembodied manhood to pass into Hades. In the fullest sense, therefore, he underwent the dissolution of death.

Similarly, in the fullest sense he overcame it. Hades had no warrant to imprison that sinless One. The grave had no right to disintegrate that undefiled body. As the apostle Peter said in his Pentecost sermon, "It was not possible that he should be holden" (Acts 2:24, KJV) of death. Our Lord's resurrection is not only an historical actuality, but it was also a moral necessity. Death had no right to him; for although he had died a judicially vicarious death as Sinbearer on behalf of others, he himself was utterly sinless. Satan was foiled. Death, which had impatiently claimed the crucified Messiah as its victim, now suddenly became powerless to hold him. Satan had expended all his arts and wiles of temptation upon the guileless Man of Galilee and had failed. Jesus, the second Adam, had proved himself—even in his human nature—morally stronger than Lucifer.

So now Jesus the victim became Jesus the victor. He wrested from Diabolos the keys of Hades. Then, with this victorious new authority, he vacated Hades and entered the sepulchre where his own corpse lay. He reoccupied and reanimated his crucified body and reappeared on earth to his astonished disciples. Yes, indeed, in that sense Jesus defeated and destroyed and "abolished" death when he utterly broke its power over himself.

But further: our Lord also abolished death inasmuch as he destroyed its hold over *his people.* His resurrection-victory was not for himself alone but on behalf of those whom he died to redeem. When he rose, he thereby nullified in advance the power of death over all those human beings who should afterward become united by faith to him as their Savior.

This means, for one thing, that, when we Christian believers now die, we do not pass, as do other disembodied human souls, into the prison of Hades. We are transported into the immediate presence of

Christ in the heavenly homeland. That is what Paul declared in 2 Corinthians 5:8 (KJV), "To be absent from the body [is] to be present with the Lord." That is why he says in Philippians 1:21 (KJV), "For me to live is Christ, and to die is gain." That is why he adds, in another verse, "Having a desire to depart and to be with Christ, which is far better" (v.23). In that sense our Lord has so effectually abolished death that the grave is no longer the gloomy vestibule to Hades but the friendly portal to heavenly rapture.

Even though at present, when Christian believers depart from this world, their bodies must lie for a while in the grave, or in other ways become disintegrated, that is a permitted and overruled expedient for the benefit of the believer. If it should be asked why our Lord does not give us deathless bodies here and now, the answer is a ready one. If he were to give us immortality here and now, he would deprive us of testings, disciplinings, and tutorings which are preparing us for high destiny through "ages to come." Some of the most spiritually educative lessons we can ever learn are those which can come to us only while we are in these *mortal* bodies.

If our Lord were to clothe all his people with immortal bodies as soon as they became converted to him, the ordinary ongoings of human history would be rendered impossible. To mention just one aspect of this: our future resurrection body will not be a "flesh and blood" body; which means that although it will have real corporeality, it will be sexless and nonpropagating. A moment's reflection will show us that if our Lord were all the while interrupting the natural course in order to give his people immortal bodies immediately, history in the ordinary sense could scarcely go on.

Our Lord came to save the fallen posterity of Adam. You and I are still members of the Adamic race; and as long as the Adamic regime continues, the grave, by divine permission, will claim our mortal bodies. But, as we have said, in the case of Christian believers, this concession to the grave is only temporary. When our Lord returns to this earth in the whelming splendor of his Second Advent, "the trumpet shall sound, and the dead shall be raised incorruptible" (1 Corinthians 15:52, KJV). That is the superclimax for which we Christians wait. In an historical sense it is still future. History, however, in the sense of successive centuries, is merely an accommodation to finite human thinking. In the more fundamental sense the resurrection of the saints is already as good as done. Nothing can cancel its fulfillment because in the deepest sense of all, when Jesus rose nineteen hundred years ago, he "abolished death" once for all.

Glance now at some other words in the passage we have been considering. Our Lord Jesus "abolished death, and hath brought *life* and *immortality* to light through the gospel" (2 Timothy 1:10, KJV, italics added). Are those two words, "life" and "immortality," tautologous—two words for the same thing? I think not. The word "life" here indicates the fact, the reality, the continuity of life beyond the grave. Our Lord's resurrection has settled that beyond any further doubt.

But that other word, "immortality," fills in the *meaning* of yonder life beyond our present boundaries. The Greek word here translated "immortality" in the Authorized Version is rendered "incorruptibility" in the English Revised and the American Standard and other versions. It means "that which never withers, never decays." It occurs in 1 Corinthians 9:25, where Paul says that the crown awaiting the Lord's faithful servants, at last, is a crown never decaying. The same word reappears in 1 Corinthians 15:51-55, where we are told that "in a moment, in the twinkling of an eye," when Christ returns, "the dead shall be raised *incorruptible,*" that is, in life never withering, never decaying, never ending.

Think of it—a crown which never withers nor decays! A resurrection body which never withers nor dies! A heavenly inheritance which never withers nor decays! They are all ours in Christ! Paul has all these in mind, not to mention other imperishables, when he writes, "Our Savior Christ Jesus abolished death, and brought life and *imperishability* to light through the gospel" (see 2 Timothy 1:10).

I shall never forget my first visit to Edinburgh, Scotland. I arrived by railway train at night and came up out of Waverly Station by the long ascent of stone stairs leading to the east end of Princes Street. There I stood, not knowing for the moment which way to turn. Stretching away on the far side, I saw a long line of brightly lit shops; there seemed to be nothing on the nearer side but a black void, for it was a very dark night. Then, suddenly, away to my left I saw something which held me spellbound. Out there, in the deep darkness, like a shining fairy palace suspended in space, was the floodlit, famous Edinburgh Castle!

How long I stood there admiring it I cannot recall; but I do remember the Bible text which it brought to mind. "Why," I said to myself, "if it were not for that powerful floodlighting, one would never guess that away out there in that dark blank there could ever be a picturesque castle."

That floodlighting does for Edinburgh Castle what Jesus has done in relation to death and the beyond. He has suddenly turned a flood of light on it. He has brought "life and unfading reality" to light out there beyond the grave! You find no such light in other religions, nor in modern science, nor in all the successive speculations of human philosophy.

All this, says Paul, has been brought to light "through the *gospel.*" I am not surprised that he uses that word "gospel" here, for it means "glad tidings"—and were there ever such glad tidings brought to you and me as those which the risen Lord Jesus brings to us in the gospel? The biggest of all concerns is to know this gospel and to receive this sin-atoning, death-defeating, soul-redeeming Savior. The gospel teaches me to say not only, "Jesus *died* for me" but also, "Jesus *rose* for me." His vicarious dying and his victorious rising were both on my behalf. The biggest thing of all is to know him as Savior in living experience.

THE BASIC ISSUE

DONALD BLOESCH

Why did Jesus go to the cross? Why did he suffer and die? The answer we give shows whether we are indeed evangelical Christians or simply cultural religionists, wolves in sheep's clothing. The meaning of the cross is the issue that marks the dividing line today between the true church and the false church. Even more basic, even more controversial than the two natures of Christ is the doctrine of his saving work.

Some theologians today regard Jesus primarily as an exemplar of perfected manhood who saves us by the impact of his love. The cross simply reveals the way to salvation which can be followed by all who are filled with the "spirit of love." To be saved therefore means to walk in his steps.

Others acknowledge that Jesus comes to us from God, but they hold that the reason for his incarnation was to bring us into contact with the God-consciousness already within us. Jesus is a mirror or reflection of the divinity that is in all of us.

Donald Bloesch was born in Bremen, Indiana, and was educated at Elmhurst (Illinois) College, the Chicago Theological Seminary, and the University of Chicago. He engaged in post-doctoral studies at Oxford, Basel, and Tübingen universities. He is currently professor of theology at Dubuque Theological Seminary, Iowa. He is an active writer and author, the latest of his offerings being *The Invaded Church*. He is former president of the American Theological Society.

Holy Scripture gives quite a different answer to the question. On the cross, the Son of God bore the punishment that we deserve to suffer because of our transgressions. We do not grasp the full import of the cross until we realize that Jesus died not only on our behalf but also in our place. He died as our representative or substitute. His death was a vicarious sacrifice for sin.

Theologians through the ages have depicted this as the great substitution. Christ took upon himself our sin, guilt, and shame while his righteousness and glory were imputed to us. As Paul put it, "For our sake he made him to be sin who knew no sin, so that in him we might become the righteousness of God" (2 Corinthians 5:21). Martin Luther said, "This is the mystery of the riches of divine grace for sinners, for by a wonderful exchange our sins are now not ours but Christ's, and Christ's righteousness is not Christ's but ours." In the words of the German pietist of the eighteenth century, Nikolaus von Zinzendorf, "We are reconciled to God, not by our own works, not by our own righteousness, but wholly and solely by the blood of Christ."

In a gospel song I wrote some time ago, I sought to proclaim the Good News which we see in the sufferings and death of Jesus Christ. I titled the song "It's Good to Be Alive." It is good to be alive not because of the infinite possibilities within man or the fundamental goodness of humankind (a belief I do not share) but because of the infinite compassion of a holy and all-powerful God.

It is good to be alive because Jesus Christ was crucified. It is good to be alive because on the third day he rose from the dead, thereby demonstrating and confirming his victory over sin, death, and the devil. It is good to be alive because on the day of Pentecost the risen Christ sent forth his Holy Spirit upon his church, converting it into a mighty army. It is the Holy Spirit who sprinkles us with the blood of Christ (1 Peter 1:2), thereby empowering us for full-time kingdom service.

Do we not have to do something for our salvation? Do we not have to suffer too? No, we do not have to do anything to procure salvation. Christ has borne the terrible judgment of God in our stead. He has paid the price of sin. His atoning work is finished (John 19:30). That is the glory of the cross, for it gives all the credit, all the glory, to the merciful and holy God himself. We do not have to earn his forgiveness, for this is impossible; yet his forgiveness does not become a reality in our lives until we repent and believe.

Some who have been influenced by the human potential

movement contend that we must first accept ourselves before we can realize any kind of peace with God or our fellows. Or it is said that we must first love ourselves before we can enter into a loving relationship with anyone else. While there is some truth in this on the purely horizontal plane, it is not the gospel.

The gospel is that God loves us even when we are unable to love ourselves, even when we are incapable of accepting ourselves. His love reaches out to us despite our sense of unworthiness. His grace breaks through our defenses even before we can respond in faith and love. His grace awakens a response of love within us which was not possible hitherto.

I have said that Jesus has done it all. But this does not mean that we do not have to do anything at all! We must believe and accept this salvation that has been won for us. We must receive the riches of God's mercy in faith, as the apostle Paul says. And faith is not simply assent to a creedal dogma; it is a total commitment.

The Christian in following his Lord no longer has to suffer penalties for sins; that has been taken care of by Christ. Now he undergoes disciplines which equip him for Christian service. He suffers the travail of faith but not the guilt of sin; he bears the yoke of Christ (Matthew 11:29-30) but not the curse of the law. Our good deeds are a sign of and a witness to the justification which is ours through faith. They proclaim the saving work of Christ which alone saves us from sin, death, and hell. Our good works are an evidence and consequence of a living faith in the only Savior, Jesus Christ.

It is not required of us to work out our karma or burden of guilt, as envisioned in Hinduism and Buddhism. Jesus Christ has borne our karma, and we need only to acknowledge and proclaim the fact. He has reaped the hell and agony we have sown (Isaiah 53:5-6). Because of his sacrifice, what is sown in dishonor will be raised in glory (1 Corinthians 15:43). Heaven is not finally attained after successive reincarnations either in this world or in some other world. The glory of heaven is available now and needs only to be received by faith. This glory in its fullness lies before us, but now we have a foretaste of it in the decision and surrender of faith (Romans 8:23; 1 Peter 5:1).

Grace is a wonderful word in the New Testament and indeed through the whole of Scripture. Basically it means the undeserved favor of a loving God. The grace of God is the compassion of God for lost sinners. When we say that we are saved by grace, we mean that we are saved exclusively by the hand of the righteous and loving God.

Even our faith is a gift of grace; we can respond to the offer of salvation only through the work of the Spirit upon us and within us. God's grace, moreover, is costly. It is free, but it is not cheap. It cost God the very life of his own Son. It must cost us our lives, our treasures, our time, even our reputations, as we follow Jesus Christ in obedience and discipleship.

Salvation is a writ of pardon. Our debts have been paid by the Judge himself. Yet we must accept this, believe in this, and act upon this. We must live in outgoing love and joyous gratitude because of this. May we glorify him in our words and actions! May we live and die to the glory of God!

BEHIND THE BRONZE DOORS OF CALVARY

JAMES M. BOICE

What did Jesus Christ think about as he hung upon the cross? What did he think about during the three hours when he was made sin for mankind?

The answer to this question is not obvious in Scripture, for the hours of darkness were private hours in which God shrouded his Son from man's gaze. There had been public hours when Jesus moved slowly among the poor and paused to teach his disciples. There had been public hours even on the day of crucifixion as Jesus spoke to the soldiers, committed his mother to the care of John, and assured the repentant thief of Paradise.

But at twelve o'clock this changed. At that hour a great darkness that lasted until three o'clock in the afternoon covered the land; at this time Christ cried out commending his spirit into the hands of the Father.

These three hours were much like the moments when the car bearing the body of Senator Robert Kennedy arrived at St. Patrick's Cathedral in New York for his funeral. The body was placed before

---

James Montgomery Boice is the radio preacher of "The Bible Study Hour." This broadcast originates in Philadelphia, Pennsylvania. He also serves as pastor of the Tenth Presbyterian Church of the same city. Besides his heavy involvement in preaching, he finds time to write. He serves as consulting editor to *Eternity,* to which he contributes frequently. He also has written several books, among them a two-volume *Exposition of the Gospel of John.*

---

the altar, and the bronze doors of St. Patrick's were shut. That was a time for the family. No other eyes disturbed their privacy. Later, millions could see the scene by television, not only in this country but also around the world. But for those first few moments it was a private, family time.

In the same way, from noon until three o'clock on the day we now call "Good Friday," God shut the bronze doors of heaven upon Jesus Christ, and what transpired there was between God the Father and God the Son alone.

There is no reason why we ought to know what Jesus thought about during those three hours. God need not have revealed it to us. And yet, he has—by means of certain clues in Scripture.

The first clue is that Jesus Christ cried out with a loud voice at the beginning of the period of darkness, "My God, my God, why hast thou forsaken me?" (Mark 15:34), a direct quotation of Psalm 22:1.

The second clue is that at the end of the three hours Jesus cried out again, saying, "It is finished" (John 19:30). This phrase is a quotation of the last verse of the psalm (Psalm 22:31). The English-speaking reader will not find this phrase in the English translation of the psalm, but it is a legitimate translation of the one Hebrew word that occurs there. The verse itself can read, "They shall come, and shall declare his righteousness unto a people that shall be born, that it is finished."

Do you see what this implies? It seems that during the three private hours the mind of Christ traversed the scope of the psalm. He thought of the alienation of the One who was made sin for mankind. He passed on to reflect on the description of suffering that the psalm includes. He thought of the final section that speaks of the spread of the gospel among the Gentiles. Only after that did Jesus utter the phrase that marks the psalm's Hebrew ending.

In this psalm there are three pictures of Christ that partially explain his suffering.

The first verse speaks of Christ as forsaken. When I was young, I read a book that suggested that Jesus really was not forsaken by God, that he only imagined he was forsaken. It taught that Jesus almost lost his faith in God, but that he recovered it later when he knew that God had sustained him. I later learned that this book was wrong. It was nonsense! Christ was bearing the penalty for sin, which is death (Romans 6:23), and death means separation from God.

What is death? Certainly not physical death alone, but spiritual death. And spiritual death is the separation of the soul from the source of life which is God. And when Christ cried out in a loud voice, "My God, my God, why hast thou forsaken me?" it was the cry of one actually abandoned by the Father.

You and I can never pretend fully to understand this. We cannot imagine how there could have been a division in the Godhead. How can God the Son be forsaken by God the Father? It is a great mystery. But it is true nevertheless. Christ was forsaken. And by it Jesus accomplished our salvation.

The second picture comes from verse 6 (Psalm 22): "I am a worm, and no man; scorned by men, and despised by the people." Why a worm? Why this unusual image?

To understand this verse, one must realize that the Hebrew word for worm had actually come to refer almost exclusively to a special worm from which the people of the Near East derived a valuable crimson dye. It was much like an insect that exists in Mexico today called the "cochineal." The worm was the tola, and the dye was formed from its blood, released when the animal was crushed. In Hebrew the word for scarlet literally means "the splendor of the tola."

The tola is referred to several times in Scripture. It is the worm that spoiled the manna in the wilderness. The scarlet dye for the linen of the wilderness tabernacle came from the blood of the tola. It is said of Saul in Second Samuel that he dressed the women of Israel in scarlet; that is, he introduced a period of such prosperity that their robes could be dyed by the tola.

All of this throws an illuminating light upon this psalm. For when Jesus thought of himself as the tola, he thought of himself as the worm who is crushed for God's people. His blood was shed for us that we might be clothed in bright raiment.

The third image refers to execution. The psalm says, "Save me from the lion's mouth; for thou hast heard me from the horns of the unicorns" (v. 21, KJV). The animal mentioned is not really a unicorn, for a unicorn does not exist. Actually it is a type of wild ox with long, pointed horns to which victims were sometimes bound for execution. As Jesus thought about this image, he must have thought about the forensic aspects of his death and remembered that God was putting him to death for others' sin.

Jesus forsaken! Jesus crushed! Jesus executed! All these help to explain his crucifixion.

These pictures are wonderful, but there is a better one to come.

Before his crucifixion Jesus thought only of other people. From noon until three in the afternoon his mind turned to the meaning of his suffering. But his thoughts did not end there. He did not stop with the subject of his suffering. Instead, his mind turned back again to other people, and he went on to think of the fruit of his work in those who would later become Christians.

First he thought of his disciples. Immediately after the verse that speaks most clearly of Christ's death, the psalm goes on to say, "I will declare thy name unto my brethren; in the midst of the congregation will I praise thee" (v. 22, KJV). Not long before his crucifixion Jesus prayed for his disciples—in the long prayer recorded in John 17. Now, even while he was dying, he thought of them again. Before, they had been only his followers. Now they were brethren. By his death they were to become sons of God and coheirs with him of God's glory.

Finally, Jesus looked to the spread of the gospel beyond his disciples, beyond Judaism, to the Gentiles. Have you ever noticed the interesting contrast between verses 22 and 25? Verse 22 says, "I will declare thy name . . . in the midst of the congregation." Verse 25 says, "My praise shall be of thee in the great congregation."

The second verse undoubtedly speaks of the spread of the gospel to us, for the psalm goes on to say, "All the ends of the world shall remember and turn unto the Lord, and all the kindreds of the nations shall worship before thee."

That verse is wonderful to me, for I am included in that number. And so are you, if you are a believer in the Lord Jesus Christ. Christ was thinking of you as he hung upon the cross. He died for you personally. If you are not a believer in Jesus, I can tell you that he wants you to come to him as many others have done. It may help you to know that in the moment of his death he looked forward to the spread of the gospel among the Gentiles. And his soul was satisfied.

HE COULD HAVE SAVED HIMSELF

BOB W. BROWN

The world always assumes that a man will save himself if he can. Thus we still are awed by the sacrifice of men like the four chaplains who gave away their life jackets and went down on the sinking *Dorchester* during World War II.

The enemies of Jesus revealed this assumption when they challenged him to save himself and come down from the cross. When he refused to leave the cross, they shouted, "He saved others; he cannot save himself" (Mark 15:30-31). This was a logical deduction on their part, but it was false. He could have saved himself, but he refused to.

Jesus could have saved himself by the simple expedient of staying away from Jerusalem. His ministry in Galilee was successful; and although harassed by the Pharisees' investigating committee, misunderstood by people in his hometown, and living the life of an itinerant, he was not in real danger.

Surely there was enough to do in Galilee. All of the sick there

---

Bob W. Brown received his education from Georgetown College and Southern Baptist Theological Seminary. He has held Kentucky pastorates in Covington, Louisville, and presently Trinity Baptist Church of Lexington. In addition to his busy pastoral activities he finds time to do evangelistic work and writing. His books include *It's Been One of Those Days, Lord, How Can We Get Lily Rose to Settle Down?* and *The Church Is People.* He has also written many articles for various periodicals.

hadn't been healed. All of the diseased weren't cured. All of the sinners weren't saved. There was enough work to do in Galilee to keep him busy for another five years. Perhaps by then things in Jerusalem would have calmed down. Was there any reason to agitate his enemies? He could have just "laid low" for awhile, and things should have gotten better.

But Jesus didn't stay where it was safe. With determination and courage he set his face steadfastly toward Jerusalem. He went with resolute step toward the area of conflict and the cross. They would not have to pursue him in the hills of Galilee. He would challenge them by his presence.

On the night of his arrest in Gethsemane he could have saved himself by running away. The idea of Jesus' running away is shocking, but it would have been a way of escape. Most of the Twelve ran away when the soldiers came to the garden. It was dark. Jesus was warned that the soldiers were coming. He could have fled in the night. After all, Paul was let down over the wall by night, and who accuses him of cowardice?

There was another consideration in the garden. If he yielded to the arrest and trial, he was recognizing the authority and power of a corrupt and perverted system of law. In fact he had exposed, criticized, and opposed these people and their laws for more than three years. To yield to their arrest would be tacitly to approve their authority. With this kind of rationale, running away would have made sense.

No one today would criticize a man who fled from arrest in China or Cuba. Jesus was no criminal. The arrest and subsequent trial were illegal, and he didn't have a fair chance. He was convicted before the trial and he knew it! Reason enough to run away.

Yet he submitted to the soldiers. Others, such as Stephen and Huss and Paul Carlson, would follow him, they wouldn't run away either.

So he went down to the trial, a prisoner. Another chance to save himself was lost. But he couldn't save himself and save us, too.

From the account it is apparent that Governor Pilate wanted to turn him loose. There were several reasons. The governor didn't want to cooperate with the Jewish leaders. Jesus really seemed harmless enough, a bit of a dreamer, but harmless. Pilate wasn't afraid of kingdoms in other worlds and might have enjoyed a discussion on the question of "What is truth?" Probably the governor had a sense of justice, too, and he knew that by Roman law Jesus hadn't done anything worthy of death. And, of course, Pilate's wife was intensely afraid of this man and the trial.

Jesus could have saved himself by reasoning with the governor. And what was wrong with that? He had a good case to make. He had done no wrong. In fact, he had discouraged a revolution by the sword. He had encouraged the people to be meek, temperate, and loving. He had said to walk a second mile. Nothing frightening to a despot in that kind of talk.

Pilate saw no legal fault in him. That sounds like a passport to freedom—if Jesus would just plead his case. Tell the governor about turning the other cheek and giving alms and forgiving seventy times. Surely the governor would free him.

Of course, to be totally honest, he must also tell the governor that men are to be free—and that in his kingdom there is no place for rank, pomp, or force; that there is no class system, no hierarchy, or privilege—a kingdom without governors, if you please. This kind of kingdom would hardly appeal to the Roman, but a man at least should make an attempt to save himself.

Most of us know how to live in two worlds: we become adept at rationalizing with the powers that be. Surely Jesus could be as clever as we are. A little diplomacy now in the governor's hall! Perhaps even some inferences about the Jewish authorities; Pilate didn't think much of them. Some sophisticated humor; make a good impression on Pilate and he can save himself. But then he couldn't save us.

Pilate appealed to the crowd: "Shall I release unto you Jesus or Barabbas?" The carpenter had another chance to save himself. He was a national hero. Just a few days before, on Palm Sunday, the same crowd had been singing, waving palm branches, calling him "King." Had they really changed that much in five days?

As he stood there on the balcony looking down on the crowded streets, Jesus had a golden opportunity to save himself. He knew how to speak to a multitude. Once he had spoken to more than five thousand. He had a chance to appeal to the people, a jury of thousands.

Had they forgotten the lame who walked, blind who saw, lepers who were made whole? He could have reminded them. He could have recalled for them the loaves and fishes. Public speakers had been reciting their accomplishments for four thousand years for less reward than their own lives. This was language the crowd would have understood—bread, health, peace. Why didn't he just ask them for his life?

Jesus—you should have told them what you could have done for them, that you hadn't ever harmed anyone. You should have promised them healing. Called attention to your wounds. How much did they want? A scourging was enough. You could have gone home to Galilee. Bound your wounds, rested. There is always another day. You should have asked the crowd for mercy. Why did you stand in silence before them? You should have appealed to the crowd.

He could have saved himself by asking the street crowd for his life. But, of course, he couldn't have saved us.

Finally, he was the Son of God. The winds and waves obeyed his voice. He could calm a storm, turn water into wine, straighten a twisted limb, cure a leper, raise Lazarus. He was the Creator of it all and had perfect dominion over all. They couldn't take his life; he was God and he had to lay it down. He could have saved himself by using his divine power.

He could have called for an army of ten thousand angels and reduced the Roman legions to paper dolls. He could have struck Pilate and the screaming crowd dumb. He could have changed the cross to a willow sapling . . . turned nails into blades of grass . . . the scourging whip into a flower stem.

The world had never really accepted him. No room when he was born. No place to lay his head. Betrayed by Judas, denied by Peter, misunderstood by mother and brothers. Three times they tried to stone him. His hometown neighbors tried to push him off a cliff. He was harassed constantly by religious men who wouldn't see nor hear.

Then a final pompous effrontery. They were going to kill him. Frail and foolish men who had spit in his face, tried him by night, bought off his friend, and feared him. They trudged out to Golgotha, thinking that victory was in their greedy grasp. They would kill him and return to business as usual. The egotism of it!

Just a lightning bolt now, Lord. Or at least a mighty earthquake. You should have let them know that you *do* have power over men with evil design. How could a good God let this kind of evil win? Weren't you afraid that, if you didn't put them down by divine power, your followers would all panic and run? There would be nothing left. You made a good start. Jesus, why did you give up? Why didn't you call the angels? Wipe them out? Come down from the cross? We can believe only in one who wins.

Waited for the third day? But why? You should have saved yourself and come down from the cross.

"He saved others; he cannot save himself" (Matthew 27:42).

"For Christ also died for sins once for all, the righteous for the unrighteous, that he might bring us to God" (1 Peter 3:18).

DEPERSONALIZATION AND RESURRECTION FAITH

MYRON R. CHARTIER

In the film *Dr. Zhivago* there is a scene in which Strelnikov and Yuri Zhivago discuss Yuri's poetry and his future private life in Varykino, and two short sentences from that scene have burned a brand-like impression upon my mind. Strelnikov, in reacting to Yuri's poetry and ambitions, says, "The personal life is dead in Russia. History has killed it."

I wanted to reject the implications of these words, but deep inside I realized something of their meaning, not only for Russia but also for all contemporary life. For we live in a world that seeks to strip us of the personal. The forces of our age appear to make life look absurd, to undermine the sense of purpose in existence.

What are the forces of depersonalization in our time? There are at least four, and the Christian believer can scarcely enumerate them without sensing the dramatic counterforce of the resurrection message.

One depersonalizing factor has been the scientific revolution.

Myron R. Chartier received his education at the University of Colorado, Kansas State College, and California Baptist Theological Seminary. He received his Ph.D. from the University of Denver. He served as professor of communication at the American Baptist Seminary of the West at Covina, California. He is now professor of ministry at Eastern Baptist Seminary, Philadelphia. He is the author of a number of articles dealing with speech and communication.

Science has given man the objective method, and man has been able to assert his power and authority over the materials of his world. The mountains have yielded their iron, gold, and uranium. The power of water has been harnessed. The oceans have been imprisoned within the lines of latitude and longitude, and the wonder of air has been captured by the isobars of the meteorologist. Man is the undisputed ruler of his world.

But this same tool with which he has split the atom and invaded space is also the weapon that threatens man himself. For he is a part of the world he seeks to dominate. The process by which he elevates himself to the position of the lord of the whole earth informs him that he is merely a temporary chemical episode in the life of one of the minor planets. Man has organized his world into categories of thingness so he can force it to serve his imaginative desires, but in the process he has discovered that he himself is a thing. The king on the throne of the universe finds himself just another statistic.

A second force threatening the personal is the population explosion. In a sense this is the problem of our age. Sir Julian Huxley, the distinguished English biologist, says it raises the whole question, "What are people for?" He points out that the tremendous increase in the quantity of people "is increasingly affecting the quality of their lives and their future, and affecting it almost wholly for the worse."[1] Georg Borgstrom, professor of food science at Michigan State University, has declared, "As things now stand we seem to face the alternative of nuclear annihilation or universal suffocation."[2]

With a world on the edge of famine it seems somewhat shortsighted to get greatly excited about individual freedom, civil rights, student rights, and human dignity. Until the population problem is solved, we will continue to be threatened by a growing impersonalness. Our lives will become more and more regimented merely for the sake of survival. Government will almost inevitably become bigger and bigger. We will become increasingly subjected to the IBM numbers game and the mentality of thingness.

Another depersonalizing force is one we impose on ourselves. Each of us is at times guilty of self-inflicted depersonalization. Refusal to involve ourselves deeply with other persons can

[1] Julian Huxley, ed., *The Humanist Frame* (New York: Harper & Row, Publishers, 1962), p. 24.

[2] Georg Borgstrom, *The Hungry Planet* (New York: Macmillan, Inc., 1965), p. viii.

depersonalize us as human beings. Reuel Howe has written in *The Miracle of Dialogue,* "Communication means life or death to persons."[3] Many of us find it hard to enter into more than superficial relationships with others. Therefore we feel cut off from the intimacy that makes life significant. Self-revelation is indeed difficult, often dangerous, for it is easy to be misunderstood. There are times when we want to reveal to another person our anxieties, our fears, our sins, our hopes, our ambitions, but we are afraid of what he may think. We are afraid he won't accept our ideas, or will laugh at us. We know from experience that this can happen; we have known what it is to be misunderstood and rejected. And so we have withdrawn into our separate boxes, hiding our true selves from other persons. In this withdrawal we find ourselves even more miserable.

Communication with others is made difficult because of our broken relationship with God. Our sinful condition imposes upon us a style of life that alienates and separates us from our brothers. Fear, suspicion, and anxiety cripple our ability to reveal ourselves to others. At a certain point in a relationship we may break the communication out of fear of being known. Or the other person may withdraw, frightened by the forthcoming revelation.

The ultimate force that seeks to depersonalize us is physical death, which cuts us off from other persons and from the physical world and brings an end to what we know of the self. We would like to take the inevitable fact of death calmly—to regard it as mere cessation of conscious reality. But the thought brings shock and terror. Unless there is life beyond this present life, life seems void of meaning. What was the point of existence for a five-year-old child smashed by a speeding car or slain by a Viet Cong terrorist or burned to death by napalm? If life's end is merely the coffin, what value is one person's life in the midst of the history of man?

The pretensions of scientism, the startling increase of population, the fear of self-revelation, and the prospect of death—these all lend support to Strelnikov's affirmation that the "personal life is dead. . . . History has killed it."

Where are we to find hope in this prospect of despair? Our hope lies in the central fact of the Christian faith—the resurrection of Jesus Christ. "I am the resurrection and the life; he who believes in me, though he die, yet shall he live, and whoever lives and believes in me

[3]Reuel Howe, *The Miracle of Dialogue* (New York: The Seabury Press, Inc., 1963), p. 4.

shall never die" (John 11:25-26). In the person of the resurrected Christ, we encounter one who has overcome the power of death. Jesus Christ, the strong Son of God, defeated the ultimate depersonalizing force, physical death. The power that raised him from the dead can overcome the forces of depersonalization in our age.

In an age when scientism seems to reduce individual existence to non-meaning, Jesus Christ, the risen Son of God, provides a different type of criterion for meaning. In him I, a weak human being, see the authentic man, the complete man. I find in him the possibility of my own completed manhood. Christ points to the personal in the midst of the impersonal.

The resurrected Christ also has made possible the Christian church. His resurrection awakened within the beaten disciples the possibility and the reality of community. The Christian church, when it is at its best, is a community of concerned people who care about individual persons. It is a community that provides an atmosphere of accepting love in which persons can feel free to be who they really are, to express their fears, their hates, their ambitions, their loves. In this impersonal age the church can offer the quality of the personal, because it stems from Christ's victory over the powers of death and depersonalization. And because of this concern for the personal in human life, Christians must take a lead in becoming informed about population problems and begin trying to find solutions.

Also, the resurrected Christ gives us the ability to have meaningful relations with other men. The unregenerate man often uses other people for his own advancement or gratification. He does not have genuine encounters with other persons, and so he often feels terribly alone, isolated from other human beings. However, union with the resurrected Christ makes it possible for one to become a real person—one who lives in open relationships with others. For indeed, Christ provides the way to other men's lives. A person in union with Christ is free to reveal himself to others because he has been accepted by God. He need no longer be afraid to risk the chance of involving himself with another person, for his most important relationship—with God—has been made secure by his faith in Christ. God's total acceptance of a person frees him to become a real person to others.

Finally, Christ's resurrection makes possible our own resurrection from the dead. The entire message of the gospel is that sin and death in Christ have been defeated. Death no longer has dominion over men, for Christ in his death and resurrection defeated the powers of death. Death need not be a depersonalizing force; the risen Christ is indeed the resurrection and the life. He holds out the promise of eternal life with God to all his disciples. The resurrection is our hope.

For some the personal may be dead, but for the children of God it is very much alive and present in the Son of God. The resurrected Christ, through his church, through our union with him, and through his own resurrection power provides a conquering force over the depersonalizing forces of our age. If we want to experience the personal in our own lives, we must meet Jesus Christ. In him we discover what it means to be a person. When we meet him, we are known and we know; we are loved and we love; we are accepted and we accept. To experience the personal is to experience the resurrected Christ at work within us.

THE SUFFERING SAVIOR

EDMUND P. CLOWNEY

Spiked to a cross beam on a hilltop, he cries, "My God, my God, why have you forsaken me?"

Who is the abandoned sufferer choking in the dust of death? His name is nailed above him: "Jesus the King of the Jews." Jesus—"the Lord is salvation." That was his name and that was his claim, but people laughed at both. "Save yourself!" they shouted at him. "Come down from the cross, Messiah, and we will believe you." But only his blood flowed down from the cross.

After two thousand years the same rage burns against the promise of his name. If Jesus is Savior, where is his salvation? Can nailed hands feed the hungry or deliver the captive? He endures anguish, but what does he do to end it? Jesus suffers; Jesus dies; but what can it mean that Jesus saves?

The gospel is still God's foolishness, wiser than men; God's weakness, stronger than men. At the cross God reveals the meaning

---

Edmund P. Clowney serves as president of Westminster Theological Seminary, Philadelphia. He received his education from Wheaton College, Westminster Seminary, and Yale Divinity School. An ordained member of the Orthodox Presbyterian Church, Dr. Clowney has served pastorates in Hamden, Connecticut, and various other places. He wrote the "Eutychus and His Kin" column for *Christianity Today* for a length of time and has written a number of books, including *Preaching and Biblical Theology* and *Called to the Ministry.*

---

of human misery, and at the cross God brings the reality of his salvation.

Misery! The thorns, the lash, the nails do not measure it. Rather the depth of agony is in Christ's cry: his Father has forsaken him. All human misery expresses our lostness from God. Before the jaws of death man tastes a dread that is the shadow of God's image. Agony no less than ecstasy reminds us that God made us for himself. That is why poets and philosophers can discern a tragic grandeur in man's misery. But the psalmist has another view. Standing before God, he sees tragedy not as man's fate but as his judgment: "For we are consumed by thine anger, and in thy wrath we are troubled. Thou has set our iniquities before thee, our secret sins in the light of thy countenance" (Psalm 90:7-8, KJV).

Man is not an innocent victim but a guilty rebel. He has defied God, corrupted his good gifts, and despised his law of love. Calvary makes that plain: the sin condemned there is not the sin of the Sufferer but the sin of those who mock his agony. And who are they? Not harlots and thieves, but religious leaders. And what turns their complacent moralism into murderous madness? Nothing but their recognition of their Victim. The hated one is the Holy One. Sinners mangle, mock, and murder him.

At the cross sin is revealed as the Bible describes it: pervading the whole man and the whole of mankind. "There is none righteous, no, not one: There is none that understandeth . . . that seeketh after God" (Romans 3:10-11, KJV). From the first sin of the first man to the final blasphemy of Antichrist all sin is against God, and no man escapes its deadly bias. We share Adam's guilt and rejoice to outdo our fathers in profligate apostasy. Even men's call for justice is self-justifying. They approach the bar of justice only to cry, "Crucify him!"

Yet man's sin does not triumph at Calvary. God's grace triumphs there. Listen to Jesus as the hour of the cross nears: "Now is my soul troubled; and what shall I say? Father, save me from this hour: but for this cause came I unto this hour. Father, glorify thy name . . ." (John 12:27-28).

How can the crucifixion glorify God's name? Can God be praised for not saving his own Son? Does not the unanswered cry "Why?" of God's Beloved on the cross bring shame rather than glory to the Father who abandoned him? Is this the faithfulness of the God who promised, "I will not fail thee, nor forsake thee"?

God the Father was never more faithful to his Son or to himself than in the darkness that covered Calvary. He did not forget his Son; God glorified his own name when he took the name of Jesus from the cross and set it above every name in heaven and earth. But the glory of Christ's resurrection victory is God's seal on the mystery of the cross.

The Father's love was not only reflected at Calvary, but it also burned with consuming fire in the darkness. At the cross the Father paid the price of love. In the heart of the infinite, eternal, unchangeable God lies the deepest mystery of suffering. The Father's love for sinners moved him to pay the price of sin himself by offering the Son of his love for enemies under his wrath. "For God so loved the world, that he gave his only begotten Son" (John 3:16).

Those who shake their fists at God for permitting suffering in the world are blind to the love of Calvary. Not only does God's love share human misery at the cross, but also God's love bears the sin that is the root of human misery. The Rock that is smitten at Calvary is the heart of God.

God's Son entered glory by way of the cross; God calls many sons and daughters to glory by the same path. The crowds that followed Jesus refused the way of the cross. They sought political solutions: armed revolt, an end to suffering, Messianic miracles to destroy the Roman armies and bring in the kingdom of Israel. Jesus refused their swords, nor would he bring in earth's judgment day with twelve legions of angels. That judgment day will come. God's justice delayed is not justice denied. The resurrection is God's sign that he will judge the world by the Man whom the world judged (Acts 17:31).

But Christ came first not to bring the judgment but to bear it. The good Shepherd gave his life for the sheep. He holds back the day of judgment until he has brought in his other scattered sheep from the ends of the earth (John 10:11, 16).

The crucified Savior calls us to take up our cross and follow him. The way of life is a road to death: if a man seeks to save his life, he will lose it; if he loses his life for Christ's sake, he will find it. After centuries of gilding the old rugged cross, Christians are again discovering that the bottom line of witness must often be signed in blood—"we must through much tribulation enter the kingdom of God" (Acts 14:22, KJV).

But how the Christian's suffering is transformed by God's love in Christ! No longer does it bring the dread of doom, for Christ has borne our judgment, and we die as we live, in Christ. Instead, suffering is God's rod of love to correct us, his proving discipline to perfect us. We know why Christ is delaying judgment, and here in the world we can endure tribulation in hope. Above all, we can rejoice when we are counted worthy to suffer shame for Christ's name. For the sake of Christ's body, the church, we may fill up our little measure of affliction as we bear cheerful witness to his grace. Above all, we may find in the midst of suffering a closer fellowship with Christ. Along with the power of his resurrection we know the fellowship of his sufferings (Philippians 3:10). Cheered by his comfort in affliction, we may better minister to others.

Christians who remember the thirst of Christ on the cross are bound by his love to give a cup of cold water in his name. The compassion of Christ's love on the cross requires sacrificial love of all who follow him, a love that transforms each day of our lives. Like the Corinthians of old, Christians may often forget the way of the cross and behave as though they were already reigning with Christ in glory. But the Lord who was made perfect in his human nature by the things that he suffered leads us again outside the camp to bear his reproach. He purposes that we should be made like him, and by the way of the cross he leads us to himself.

THE LITERAL RESURRECTION OF CHRIST

W. A. CRISWELL

I believe Christ was bodily raised from the dead; it was a physical resurrection. This, as Paul states in 1 Corinthians 15, is at the very heart of the Christian message. The book of Acts is the glorious and triumphant news announced by the apostles. Jesus has conquered sin and death, and his resurrection is a pledge that we also shall be raised from the dead. The focal point of the attack against Christianity is sometimes against the physical resurrection of Christ. The issues at stake are so serious; the validity of the Christian message is so wrapped up in our answers; the hope of the resurrection is so dear to our hearts that we ought to examine the proofs for the literal, physical resurrection of Jesus.

I would name seven such proofs.

First, there is a harmony between the resurrection of Christ and his life, words, and work. A perfect life, filled with the truth of God, could not end in a cruel, shameful death, such as we read about in the

---

W. A. Criswell was born in Eldorado, Oklahoma, and received his education at Baylor University and Southern Baptist Seminary. He served as pastor of First Baptist Church, Chickasha, Oklahoma, and later at First Baptist Church of Muskogee in the same state. In 1944 he entered upon a fruitful and widespread ministry as pastor of the historic First Baptist Church of Dallas, Texas. He served as president of the Southern Baptist Convention from 1968 to 1970. A number of books and articles have come from his pen, including *Why I Preach the Bible Is Literally True* and *Look Up, Brother.*

New Testament, if there be a God in the universe. Is that all there is to life, goodness, beauty, and perfection? If death is the climax of a life so pure and Godlike, we are faced with an insolvable mystery, namely, the permanent triumph of wrong over right. Truth and justice are ultimately nothing. But this is not the way God has made the world, and this is not the story of Christ. According to his words and promises he was to be raised from the dead. Whenever he mentioned his death, he also mentioned his resurrection (John 2:19-21). It is not without significance that the enemies of the Lord, after he was crucified and buried and sealed in a tomb, were careful to remember that he said he would rise again (Matthew 27:63). Truly the life and words of our Lord predicate a resurrection.

Another evidence of the physical resurrection of our Lord is to be found in the empty tomb. He was buried with a huge stone placed over the entrance. It was sealed with a Roman seal, and a Roman guard was set to watch the place by day and night. Yet on the morning of the third day the body disappeared. What happened? There are two alternatives: either it was taken by human hands or it was raised by supernatural power. If the body were taken by his friends, *could* they have done it? If it were stolen, what of the grave clothes that were so carefully arranged and left in perfect order? If the body were stolen, it had to be done hastily because there was a guard watching. If the body were taken by his foes, *would* they have done it? Why do the very thing that would most likely lend itself to the support of a false rumor? How account for the silence of the Jews when they heard Peter preach a few weeks later at Pentecost? In order to contradict all that Peter said about the living Lord, the easiest and most conclusive thing they could have done would be to produce the dead body of Jesus. That would have silenced Peter and the apostles forever. There is no other explanation of the empty tomb except that God supernaturally raised his Son from the dead.

We find another sign of the physical resurrection of our Lord in the transformation of his disciples. On Friday there was sadness and hopelessness. On Sunday there was gladness. The incredulous disciples themselves were hard to convince that a miracle so triumphant and precious had restored to them their blessed Lord. They literally believed not, for joy (Luke 24:4-11). They were not looking for an immortalized Jesus. They had gone to the tomb to receive a corpse.

Another indication of the physical resurrection of Jesus can be found in the existence of the early church. Where did it come from? To the Jew, anyone hanged on a tree was cursed (Deuteronomy 21:23). Yet multitudes of Jews were led to worship him (Acts 2:41), and a great company of priests became obedient to the faith (Acts 6:7). The only explanation is the truth of the resurrection of our Lord.

Another corroboration of the resurrection of Jesus was the witness of the apostle Paul. He was outstanding both in spirit and intellect. Read his letters in the New Testament. Paul wrote of the resurrection of our Lord when many witnesses to that fact were still living and could be examined. The personal testimony of the great apostle cannot be easily discounted.

Another confirmation of the physical resurrection of Christ can be found in the Gospel record itself. There is nothing comparable in human literature to the stories of the rising of Christ from the dead. Read them for yourself. Read the story of the race of Peter and John to the tomb (John 20). Read the story of the revelation of Christ to the seven disciples by the Sea of Galilee (John 21). Read the story of the unknown Christ as he walked with the two on the road to Emmaus (Luke 24). There is a sense of reality in the unadorned testimony in all of these chapters.

Another testimony to the physical resurrection of Jesus is the response of believers then and through the centuries. When the Lord Jesus was raised from the dead, he was recognized as the same Lord whom the disciples knew in the days of his flesh, only now he was immortalized and glorified.

The Lord Jesus appeared to his disciples again and again during that forty-day period. Sometimes it was without announcement. Suddenly he was there. In the garden there he was. Down a lonely road there he was. At supper there he was. In the upper room there he was. On the seashore there he was. On the mountainside there he was. Walking up Mount Olivet there he was. As this continued for over forty days, finally the disciples no longer needed that their eyes behold him. They knew him by his presence working with them. They treasured the promise. "Behold, I am with you all the days until the consummation of the age" (see Matthew 28:20). Not a day would he be away from them to the end of the world. In prosperity and in adversity; in prison, in trial, in sickness, and in health; today, tomorrow, and forever the living Lord will be with his people. Stephen saw him when he was so bitterly assailed by those who blasphemed his name. Paul met him on the Damascus road. John saw him on the lonely Isle of Patmos. Thus it has been through the centuries and the ages. Christ is our living Lord.

Dr. W. R. White, one of God's great Christian statesmen, told of a brilliant Chinese who came to services being conducted by a missionary. The young man asked for a New Testament and was given one. Later he came to confess Christ and gave this stirring testimony:

> I took the New Testament home with me. I sat down on the floor and read it through before I did anything else. I have read the great writings of Confucius. I wanted to satisfy my hungry heart there. I knocked at the door but no answer came, for Confucius was dead. I read the message of Buddhism seeking that for which my soul so profoundly longed. I knocked at the door of Buddha but no answer came, for Buddha was dead. I read the Koran. My soul longed to find peace there. I knocked at the door but no answer came, for Muhammad was dead. I read the writings of the greatest patriots and religious leaders of the past. I knocked but no answer came. While reading this New Testament, I found that it claimed its author to be alive. I knocked at that door. I found the living Christ. He came into my soul. Here my hungry heart found peace, a peace for which it has longed.

This is the testimony of God's saints through the ages. Christ is as much alive today as in all the days of his flesh. Caesar is dead; Charlemagne is dead; Richard the Lionhearted is dead; Washington is dead; Lenin and Stalin and Karl Marx are dead. They all are dead. But Jesus is not dead! Jesus is alive, and he has with him the keys of hell and of death (Revelation 1:18).

That Christ lives today, God of very God, the Savior of the world, is a testimony of God's saints here and around the world.

One of the most moving events in the life of a man is the tragedy and triumph that overtook Dr. George W. Truett, pastor of the First Baptist Church in Dallas, Texas, for forty-seven years. In the congregation of the Dallas church was Captain J. C. Arnold of the Texas Rangers, who had become chief of police in that city. He was a humble and devoted member. One day Police Chief Arnold and Pastor Truett were quail hunting in Johnson County. Captain Arnold was walking along a few paces in front of Dr. Truett. Dr. Truett shifted his gun from one arm to the other, but in so doing the trigger on the hammerless weapon was touched. The discharge struck the police chief and mortally wounded him.

All Dallas was shocked by the death of their police officer. The pastor himself was plunged into indescribable grief. He felt that he could never preach again. His hands were stained with the blood of his dear friend, blood shed as he awkwardly and carelessly handled a gun. He shut himself off from the world, and in the black shadows he brooded and prayed and read his Bible, crying unto God.

Late one Saturday night, for the first time since the accident, he fell asleep. He dreamed that Jesus appeared as visibly and realistically as some earthly friend standing by his side. He heard the Master say, "Be not afraid; you are my man from now on." Dr. Truett awoke. He awakened his wife and told her the dream. A second time he went back to sleep, and the same vision and the same words were repeated. Again he told his wife what he had seen and heard. He went back to sleep, and the third time the same vision appeared. The Master came and spoke to him just as he did before.

On Sunday Dr. Truett returned to his pulpit to preach the gospel of the unsearchable riches of Christ Jesus. That Sunday morning the Methodist churches and the Presbyterian churches and other churches dismissed their services that they might hear the great pastor. The news swept like wildfire through the city of Dallas. One spoke to the other saying: "Truett will be in his pulpit this Sunday. Truett will be preaching Christ again today."

Thus it is that Jesus our Lord is as alive today as he was two thousand years ago. He is not dead. He is alive! He lives in our hearts, and he looks upon us from heaven.

I believe in the real, physical resurrection of Jesus. I preach it.

THE ROAD TO GALILEE

W. GLYN EVANS

One of the favorite stories of the late Dr. Will H. Houghton concerns a gentleman who stood one day looking into a store window. Standing next to him and also looking in was a little boy. It was Easter time, and in keeping with the season the shopkeeper had arranged a setting of the crucifixion.

After a while the boy turned to the man. "Them's Roman soldiers," he explained.

The man said nothing, but kept studying the window.

"And there's Jesus," the boy continued.

Still no response.

"They killed him."

By this time the man, having satisfied his curiosity, started to walk away. Then he heard a patter of young feet behind him and felt a tug on his sleeve. It was the boy.

"Mister," he said, "I forgot to tell you the most important part. He's alive again!"

William Glyn Evans was born in Wales and, after migrating to the United States with his parents, began preaching at the age of sixteen. Later he was graduated from Wheaton College, Wheaton Graduate School of Theology, and Northern Illinois University. He served pastorates in Ohio and Illinois before returning to Wheaton Graduate School to teach pastoral theology. Since 1971 he has served as a pastor of the South Shore Baptist Church, Hingham, Massachusetts. He is the author of *The Road to Power, He Has Come,* and other publications.

Many of us forget that Calvary was not the end of Jesus' career. If we think the cross finished him, we've definitely omitted a very vital part of his story.

We all know that at Calvary Jesus offered himself as the sacrifice for our sins. It was there he truly and wonderfully worked our redemption. How basic and necessary was that atoning work! Yet God never intended for Jesus to "settle down" at Calvary any more than he intends us to "settle down" there.

To put it another way. There's something for us beyond the cross just as there was something for Jesus beyond his cross. The road that led to Jesus' cross didn't dead-end there. It ran through the cross and beyond it to the other side.

Isn't that what the angel said to the women? "Go quickly, and tell his disciples that he is risen from the dead; and behold, he goeth before you into Galilee; there you shall see him . . ." (Matthew 28:7, KJV).

In God's geography, the highway to Jerusalem became the highway to Galilee. The road to Jerusalem led to bitter rejection, pain, and ultimately death. The road to Galilee was a triumphant reversal. It was the road to risen life, power, and victory.

Now Jesus is our "example" and "forerunner" in all this. As he went down the road to Jerusalem, so must we. As he later sped along the road to Galilee in vibrant resurrection life, so may we. The youngest and newest of Christians will tell you that when we commit ourselves to Christ, two things will always occur: we'll be propelled into all kinds of painful suffering and later we'll be elevated into fresh power and blessing. We discover, as Jesus discovered, that there's always an "afterward" to bitterness and despair.

Joseph Nemes found it so. In his book, *Signs in the Storm,* he tells of his attempt to escape from a Communist concentration camp behind the Iron Curtain. After weeks of harrowing danger he arrived in Austria, only to be suddenly arrested and turned once again over to the Communists. In the despairing darkness of his solitary cell he faced the ultimate—the sentence of death. Symbolically speaking, Nemes was on his cross at the end of the Jerusalem road.

But in those waiting, lagging hours that followed, God began to speak to his servant. A nominal Christian, Nemes pored over the pages of his Bible (which miraculously he was allowed to keep). An intense, insatiable hunger for God began to possess him. Overwhelming everything, even his craven fear of darkness and impending death, was the hunger for God-satisfaction. His cries and pleas echoed around the stone walls of his cell until God mercifully responded and filled the young man with waves of unutterable peace and joy.

The result? His circumstances no longer mattered! He was no longer on his cross but beyond it, far beyond it, down the road to Galilee. He followed his Savior in vibrant life and power. What the Communists did with his body no longer mattered. Victory no longer lay in the hands of the prison commandant; it lay in his heart.

But God had one more surprise for his child. On the eleventh day an officer entered the cell and announced tersely, "You are free!" Unbelievingly, Nemes stumbled out into the bright sunshine a few minutes later a free man. Legally free! Yet far more important was the spiritual freedom that God brought to him while yet in his cell. In the place where he experienced his greatest defeat, he found his greatest victory.

Let's apply this fact to ourselves. We may be facing a similar catastrophe, spiritually if not physically. The point is this—right there at the dead end, the terminus, the finis is where God breaks through and opens the road to Galilee.

Remember the disciples on the road to Emmaus? What despair! "We [hoped] that it had been he which should have redeemed Israel" (Luke 24:21). That was their nadir, their apogee, the point farthest away. But while they were at that point, Jesus came along and began to talk to them. What a Bible lesson he gave them! The theme of his discourse was that the Messiah must first suffer, then become glorified. The cross was not a terminal but a tunnel. One enters a tunnel and also emerges from it. That's what happened to the disciples on the road to Emmaus. Sorrow gave way to joy and despair to jubilant victory when they saw their risen Messiah standing before them.

How different was the enthusiasm of the disciples when compared to the bleak, dismal outlook of ordinary man! Dame Edith Sitwell expresses it this way:

> Still falls the Rain—
> Dark as the world of man, black as our loss—
> Blind as the nineteen hundred and forty nails
> Upon the Cross.

Have you ever noticed how Jesus faced his cross? The night before he died he tried to prepare his disciples for what was coming

(John 13–17). In all that discourse, try to find one note of despair in Jesus' words. Instead you will find absolute assurance, perfect optimism. Read about the Father's many mansions, Jesus' coming back for his own, the coming Comforter, the fruitful Vine, and all the rest, and you'll be convinced that Jesus never expected to stay dead. To him the cross was an open door to a glorious new thrust of the Father's plan.

Now the disciples, on the other hand, didn't see it that way. Any mention of their Master's going left them cold, to say the least. They were troubled, uncertain, doubtful. They couldn't see how a cross could be a welcome thing at all. The farther they went down the road to Jerusalem, the worse they got. They began to curse, blaspheme, deny, and finally scatter completely in a desperate attempt to evade crucifixion themselves.

The Jerusalem road is always a life-testing road. It can also be a life-shattering road. It all depends upon our point of view. Jesus was strengthened as he traveled that road because he knew that eventually his Father would land him on the road to Galilee. The disciples, without that assurance, simply fell apart.

The well-known J. C. Penney lost his fortune in the Great Depression of the 1930s. His ensuing worry propelled him slowly and steadily downward until he landed in a sanatorium. With his health shattered, Penney faced the darkest hours of his life. He expected to die. One day, as he sat in a wheelchair in his room, he heard the strains of a hymn. Some Christians were holding a service nearby, and the words of the hymn came floating down the hallway:

Be not dismayed whate'er betide,
God will take care of you;
Beneath his wings of love abide,
God will take care of you.

The hymn seemed to breathe new life into the stricken man. It whispered new hope and salvation from despair. He began to see that his condition was not permanent; his devastation was not the end. He discerned a flickering light beyond his cross and the markings of a road beyond. It was the road to Galilee.

Penney renewed his dedication to God, and his health began to recover. He soon quit the sanatorium and entered the business world again. By the time of his death many years later he was the head of one of the largest department store chains in the world. More important, his experience became an inspiration to countless numbers of people who, like himself, felt they had come to the end of everything.

The road to Galilee is not pretty sentiment; it is hard reality. After his resurrection, Christ entered into his new work. He was given "all power and authority." He was free to send his Holy Spirit into the world to universalize what he had accomplished at the cross. The after-cross ministry of Jesus, through his Spirit, was to apply all of his accrued benefits to those who would believe on him. Thus the road to Galilee became the highway of blessing to the whole world.

What does this mean to us? Basically it means that our death is not the stopping point for us. "Because I live," said Jesus, "you will live also" (John 14:19). Winston Churchill once referred to death as "that black velvet." Charles de Gaulle called it "the cold, silent, eternal dark." When his wife, Nadezhda, died, Joseph Stalin said: "She is dead, and with her have died my last warm feelings for all human beings." He saw death as life's final roadblock and, in retaliation, he vented his frustration on his fellow human beings. The Christian, however, does not see it as the final roadblock, the eternal standstill. Christ blasted through the roadblock and opened up the highway into eternity. For those who follow him there is something glorious beyond.

Jesus walked the Jerusalem road only once. He'll never walk it again. But he walks the Galilee road everlastingly.

What did he find on that Galilee road? Well, he found a disciple with flagging faith and tortured conscience. He said to him, "Lovest thou me?" and that disciple was won over to a new commitment and a new zeal. He found other disciples full of doubt and uncertainty. He said to them, "Go ye into all the world and preach the gospel" and they went! Jesus took a disordered, bedraggled group of men and transformed them into a living, throbbing organism of power. They revolutionized Jerusalem. They upended the Greek world. They brought Rome herself to the feet of the once-crucified Jesus.

Galilee is essentially a believer's road. The doubters are all on the Jerusalem side. You can't get on the Galilee road without fully committing yourself to the One who said, "I'll meet you in Galilee." And once committed, you'll find yourself throbbing with the same power that turned Simon into Cephas and Thomas into an apostle. The road to Galilee is the road on which the triumphant Christ walks with his own.

WE CELEBRATE JESUS AS LORD OF ALL

GERHARD E. FROST

He lives! God is not dead! And because he lives, we celebrate. We celebrate Jesus.

Jesus, no martyred saint or fallen hero, no frail and gentle memory, no fading echo and dimming afterglow, but living Love—victorious, strong, enduring still. We celebrate him as Lord of all. My God and King!

Death, bend your stiff neck. Bow your proud head, for we celebrate Jesus. Death, you are no match for Love. It is presumptuous to think that you can hold him fast. Your reign is broken. He lives. He has won, and in his victory your crown is struck from your head.

God is not dead. "He stirs up the people," they said. They said it about Jesus when God walked the streets of time and space for those brief years. It was true. But it was not only true then. It is true today, for he lives.

I cannot escape him, this living One. When I celebrate him, he

Gerhard E. Frost was born in Sheyenne, North Dakota, and received his education from Luther College, Luther Theological Seminary, Princeton Theological Seminary, and the University of Chicago. He held pastorates in Montana and North Dakota before becoming Professor of Bible and Religious Education at Luther College and later Professor of Practical Theology at Luther Theological Seminary in St. Paul, Minnesota. He has authored a number of books, including *The Law Perfect* and *These Things I Remember*, plus many articles.

gets me into trouble. I want to be just a face in the crowd. I want to hide, but he keeps drawing me out and I am afraid. I want to run!

Why are you such a high-voltage presence, Lord Jesus? Why must my choice be between you and my pleasant stagnation? Why can I not celebrate "in peace," in comfortable aloofness from the festering facts in our human situation? Why must you, the Prince of Peace, come as the Messenger of strife? Why? Why?

Because you live.

"He stirs up the people . . . teaching. . . ." What a frightening definition of teaching! And yet, I find it to be true. To celebrate Jesus in reflection is always to be prodded into action. To be taught by him is to be stretched, and I fight that. It hurts to be stretched. Can it be that all learning is change and change is pain?

When I listen to Jesus, I can't stop with formal mastery of facts. Fierce street fights break out along the avenues and back alleys of my mind. New thoughts engage old prejudices, and big burly lies challenge truth's right to the road. I am anxious, and again I want to run. But we celebrate Jesus, and in faith's fellowship you and I may learn to stand.

He lives! He lives! We will repeat it. Words shatter under their burden as they try to say it. All language fails, and our best doxologies break into wordless wonder and silent awe. But the Word finds words for his purpose, inadequate though they be. Though they cannot say it all, they are enough, enough for you and me.

"Blessed be the God and Father of our Lord Jesus Christ! By his great mercy we have been born anew to a living hope through the resurrection of Jesus Christ from the dead, and to an inheritance which is imperishable, undefiled, and unfading, kept in heaven for you, who by God's power are guarded through faith for a salvation ready to be revealed in the last time" (1 Peter 1:3-5).

No, God is not dead. And to you who have said this, we who celebrate Jesus quietly affirm that it is not so. If you mean that our God is hidden, that he is the God who hides in the testing circumstances of our dangerous time as he once hid in diapers and on the cross, we agree. He is not only the God who is revealed in Jesus Christ. He is the "hidden God" as well. But he is not dead.

If your intent is only to raise some questions that we may not ignore, then raise them, but not with words that mislead and even blaspheme! If your purpose is to say that we are dead to his loving approaches, say this; but do not presume to fashion a deathbed for

God. Death is death; and if God were dead, no tongue could tell it. No man could proclaim it, for it is by the creating and sustaining hand of the ever-living One that we live.

"And the third day he rose again according to the Scriptures," says our ancient creed. I come to the Scriptures in order to celebrate Jesus. I come remembering what a friend has said: that a love letter must be read for what it is; that a young woman receiving an urgent message of proposal from one who loves her will not read it as an English composition, though it is that, nor as data on courtship in our culture, though it is that, too; she will read it for what it is, a heart's expression of a great longing, the longing to be one! This is what the Bible is to me, God's message of longing and willingness, but more than that, God's news that all barriers have been broken down, that I am accepted and forgiven.

"Father." When I say that in faith and trust, I celebrate Jesus, for "When we cry, 'Abba! Father!' it is the Spirit himself bearing witness with our spirit that we are children of God, and if children, then heirs, heirs of God and fellow heirs with Christ, provided we suffer with him in order that we may also be glorified with him" (Romans 8:15*b*-16). Where there is Easter, there is Christmas and Pentecost, too. Whenever I say, either alone or with you, "Our Father," I celebrate my baptism into the body of Christ.

I know that life is single file. It is true, as Luther said, that "every man must do his own believing even as every man must do his own dying." Remembéring that there is a world of difference if I say only "he is risen" and do not affirm that he is risen for me, I place myself before his face. I build my house of life on this Rock, that "he has redeemed me, a lost and condemned creature, bought and freed me from sin, death, and the power of the devil, not with silver or gold, but with his holy and precious blood, and with his innocent sufferings and death."

Today the Lord of the church "stirs up the people." He arrests us and addresses us. He calls and sends. He asks his church to leave her sheltering walls and walk the streets with him. He uncovers long-forgotten issues. He exposes frontiers more vast than any we have ever known before. I am a member of this church, but my temptation is to "send him to Herod." I have been well schooled in this art of sending him to "someone else." I still like "truth in the sky" better than Truth in the flesh, wearing work clothes. I prefer to think of Love rather than *acts* of love and Justice rather than *acts* of justice.

In a world that is glutted on trivia and sick unto death of itself, a world starving for the daily doxology of loving service, the holy liturgy of self-giving and fellowship, we affirm: No, God is not dead. He lives. And “no one who believes in him will be put to shame.”

THE LIVING CHRIST

FRANK E. GAEBELEIN

The Easter message, despite its familiarity, remains one of the most incompletely understood of the foundations of the Christian faith. To celebrate the resurrection with flowers, music, and a special sermon is all very fitting. But as Floyd V. Filson said in *Jesus Christ the Risen Lord,* "There is a fatal weakness in our modern emphasis on Easter. The emphasis is, of course, true to the Gospel message; the resurrection is central. But too many Christians begin to look to a long summer vacation once they have had a 'big Easter.' For the first Christians, the resurrection was not the end of the story; it was the climax which leads on to further momentous developments."

Of no other great religious leader except Jesus Christ can it be said, "He shewed himself alive after his passion by many infallible proofs" (Acts 1:3, KJV). Such a thing cannot possibly be claimed for Moses, who died before entering the Promised Land. Nor can it be said of Confucius, who ended his days a disillusioned old man. Neither can it be asserted of Buddha or Lao-Tse, Zoroaster or

---

Frank E. Gaebelein has had a varied experience as educator, author, administrator, and preacher. He received his education from New York University and Harvard College. He was organizer of Stonybrook School (Long Island) and served as headmaster from 1922 to 1963. A copious writer, Gaebelein was co-editor of *Christianity Today* from 1963 to 1966 and also contributed to that magazine's column, "The Other Side." He is author of *The Pattern of God's Truth, A Varied Harvest,* and numbers of other writings.

Mohammed. They too went the way of other men, and their followers have never dared claim that they left the grave.

Christ is different. His work has a unique consummation and continuance. Just as no other religion aside from Christianity has a founder who arose from the dead, so no other religion has a founder who died for the sin of the world and who continues to save all who put their trust in him.

"But," someone says—and there are many who are saying it today—"all this is mere assertion. It's all very well to declare that Jesus Christ is unique because he alone rose from the dead. But we want more than assertion. We want proof."

There is proof if we will but look at the evidence. The resurrection of Jesus Christ does not rest on unsupported assumption. It is not a wistful grasping after some vision. On the contrary, it is based upon a whole chain of evidence—"many infallible proofs," as Luke calls them.

What are they? Well, there is the fact of the empty tomb, a fact that stands in the way of all attempts to explain away the resurrection. There is the circumstance of the precisely disposed grave clothes. There are the numerous appearances over nearly six weeks, as he was "seen of them forty days," during which he appeared to Mary Magdalene, to two disciples on the Emmaus road, to the disciples in the locked room when Thomas was present, to the seven at the Sea of Galilee, to the five hundred, to James, and to Paul on the Damascus road. These are some of the infallible proofs.

And there are also others, such as the existence of the Christian church itself. For it is undeniable that, if the disciples had not been convinced that their Lord arose and was living, there would never have been any Christian church. Dr. Josiah Penniman, a former president of the University of Pennsylvania, used to teach a course in English Bible to college students. When he was asked one day about proof of the resurrection, he quietly walked to the window of his classroom and pointed to the many church spires in that part of Philadelphia. The church is indeed a visible outcome of the fact that the Lord who is its Founder and Foundation actually rose from the dead.

Again, every Sunday bears its own witness to the living Christ. For the only adequate way to account for the shift in the day of worship from the sabbath to the First Day is the resurrection. Sunday is for Christians the Lord's Day, because on this day he arose.

Luke's emphasis on proof reminds us that the resurrection is as much a historic event as the birth in Bethlehem and the death on the cross. As the risen Christ said: "I am he that liveth and was dead: and behold, I am alive for evermore" (Revelation 1:18, KJV).

But the resurrection, while indeed historical, is also an event of continuing, contemporary significance. Important as the evidence is, the risen Christ is for us Christians more than an event of the past, more than a great theological doctrine. He is a living person, and it is our inexpressible privilege to know him personally. As Paul put it in brief but intimate words, "Christ . . . is our life" (Colossians 3:4). By this he meant that, though our Lord Jesus Christ rose once and for all in the mighty display of God's power when the stone was rolled away and his body left the grave, he keeps on living in every Christian life.

It is significant that the Bible records nine instances where human beings were raised from the dead—several of them in the Old Testament and others in the New Testament, including the raising of Jairus's daughter, the raising of the son of the widow at Nain, and, most notable of all, the raising of Lazarus. But in every case these persons were raised in their mortal bodies to continued human life after which they died. Christ was raised "after the power of an endless life" (Hebrews 7:16, KJV) in a unique, glorified, and deathless body. Moreover, his resurrected body is the "firstfruits of them that slept" (1 Corinthians 15:20, KJV), the very pattern and assurance of our own resurrection when he comes again. Therefore we are able to say in the Apostles' Creed: "I believe in the resurrection of the body."

The Easter message is the message of the living Christ. But how is he living? The answer to that question faces us with a reality that is at the same time a mystery. He lives in his glorified body. He lives in a body that transcends human limitations. When he appeared during the forty days, he had a body bearing the print of the nails and the wound of the spear. In this same body he ascended. In it he is in the place of exaltation at the right hand of God. Yet because of who he is, because he is God incarnate and so an infinite person, he is spiritually and actually beyond the limitations of time and space. So we know—we don't conjecture or guess—we Christians *know* that Christ is present with us. Just as David Livingstone in his journeys into the heart of Africa was not alone because of the promise of his Lord, "Lo, I am with you alway, even unto the end of the world" (Matthew 28:20, KJV), so we who are not exploring a continent but living everyday lives have Christ with us. It is our heritage to know and have fellowship with the risen, living Lord. God said to Hudson Taylor, "I will evangelize China, if you will walk with me." And Hudson Taylor did. He walked with God with the result that the great China Inland Mission came into being. It is the risen Christ with whom we walk.

Toward the middle of his life, R. W. Dale, the author of a classic book on the atonement, made, he said, "the discovery that Jesus is alive," and it transformed everything for him. Have you made this discovery?

"Christ," said Paul, "is our life." Or, as he put it so very personally, "Christ liveth in me" (Galatians 2:20, KJV). Think of it! Jesus Christ, by his spirit, actually lives in the believer's heart! He is identified with us and we with him. This being the case, we cannot even begin to know the fullness of the Easter truth till we learn something of what it means to have Christ living in us. These lines, attributed to St. Patrick, express it:

Christ be with me, Christ within me,
Christ behind me, Christ before me,
Christ beside me, Christ to win me,
Christ to comfort and restore me,
Christ beneath me, Christ above me,
Christ in quiet, Christ in danger,
Christ in hearts of all that love me,
Christ in mouth of friend and stranger.

But to realize these things is no sudden achievement. It was Spurgeon who said with humility, "In forty years I have not spent fifteen waking moments without thinking of Jesus." How is it with us? Do we cultivate the presence of the living Christ by thinking often of him?

When our Lord appeared to Thomas, who had doubted the reality of his resurrection, Thomas declared, "My Lord and my God." Then Jesus said to him: "Thomas, because thou hast seen me, thou hast believed: blessed are they who have not seen, and yet have believed" (John 20:28-29). That is the Easter beatitude, the beatitude of the living Christ. And it belongs to all who, looking in faith to the risen Lord, can echo the words of 1 Peter 1:8 in their hearts, "whom having not seen, ye love."

WE WALK BACKWARD INTO THE FUTURE

STUART P. GARVER

Tense and troubled by the rapid and often violent changes engulfing us, we turn to the past hoping to find some clue for the solving of our problems; yet all the while we timidly back off into the future in order to escape the horrors of the present. It is not strange, therefore, that instead of drawing strength from the past we find ourselves repeating the mistakes, miscalculations, and disasters of our forefathers. Mere copiers of other men stumble over the same stones of human perversity that destroyed their peers. That is why the style or manner of our sinning may vary from age to age, but the foolishness of the sinner is duplicated in generation after generation.

But the winds must be to the back of men who would survive the storm and face the future with confidence. The truly great ones are those who get turned around and walk into the future with heads erect and hearts thumping under the stimulus of new responsibilities as pioneers of vastly expanded horizons. It is precisely this business of turning men around that engaged the risen Christ, and nothing is more exhilarating than stories of the complete about-face which he

---

Stuart P. Garver, the editor of *Christian Heritage,* is a graduate of Philadelphia Bible College, Gettysburg College, and Gettysburg Lutheran Seminary. He has pastored several churches, taught at Barrington College, and authored a number of books, including *Our Christian Heritage, Watch Your Teaching,* and others. In addition to his editorial duties, he serves as Executive Director of Christ's Mission, Hackensack, New Jersey.

---

accomplishes in the lives of disciplined disciples of every age.

Remember how the twelve apostles backed away from him when he divulged with what evil intent his enemies would take his life? Recall how Peter, upon hearing Jesus say he must go to Jerusalem and there suffer cruel treatment and finally be put to death, awkwardly backed away into a dismal future, saying, "Far be it from thee, Lord!" (Matthew 16:22, KJV). Aghast at the very thought of crucifixion, Peter protested too loudly and subsequently had to be warned that before the cock crowed he would deny his friend thrice.

Consider, too, the sons of Zebedee who backed away from the same announcement of his death to argue which of them should be the greatest in his kingdom. Visions of grandeur are like festering carbuncles on the character of men being groomed for positions of power, such as he had envisioned for James and John. And, last of all, what are we to think of Judas who stalked backward into an horrendous affair by consorting with those who sought the Savior's blood?

Think still more of the fisherman who, after following Jesus for three glorious years, backed off into a life of despair, saying simply: "I go a fishing!" (John 21:3). And what of those who out of fear hid themselves behind locked doors or as forlorn travelers to Emmaus murmured: "We had hoped that he was the one to redeem Israel" (Luke 24:21). Every last one of them appears in Scripture as men who slink off backward from the nightmare called Calvary into a future they cannot or would not face.

All these early believers needed to be turned around.

But how?

By whom? When? Where?

The answers to these questions take us far beyond a simple Bible quiz on the events associated with his resurrection. For their turning around after his resurrection is the key to the greatest miracle of all time—the building of his church.

And what an accomplishment that is! Nations have fallen, kingdoms have crumbled, kings and rulers are vanquished; but his church, whose very foundations were established by his death and resurrection, survives and covers all the earth because he succeeded in turning men around who were strongly tempted to walk away backward into a future without Christ, without God, and worst of all, without hope.

Men may make a mockery of his church today and discount what he had accomplished through its turned-around disciples; but they cannot deny its presence. They may scorn its message and publicize its faults with sneers and jeers; but they cannot deny those whose lives are living testimonies that he still is in the business of turning men around. The very fact that his church is now established through the world, that it endures despite its foes, that it today continues to channel God's regenerating energies to men of whatever culture should cause thinking men to ponder deeply the miraculous accomplishment of the risen Savior in persuading those first disciples that there would never again be a reason for a man to walk backward into the future.

I know it is a widely held view today that the Christian church is nothing more than a vestigial organism left over from older generations but totally lacking any significant resemblance to the religion propounded by Jesus of Nazareth. Its presence is tolerated, but its power to give meaning to life is denied. I know also that there are some within the church who deplore and depreciate the viability of its ministry for modern societies. Even Jesus before his death asked: "When the Son of man cometh, shall he find faith on the earth?" (Luke 18:8, KJV). But he asked that question after exhorting them, saying, "Men ought always to pray, and not to faint" (Luke 18:1, KJV). To all such, his almost defiant reply is: "I will build my church; and the gates of hell shall not prevail against it" (Matthew 16:18, KJV).

Unfortunately humankind is all too accurately described by Pierre de Beaumarchais in his play *Le Barbier de Seville* when he has Figaro say: "I hasten to laugh at everything, for fear of being obliged to weep!" The past does draw tears—Jesus asked, "Woman, why weepest thou?"—simply because people can find no explanation for the tragedies that have overtaken them. They can only back off with an idiotic laugh knowing everything is laughable until they, or Someone, can discern an underlying purpose running through the torn fabric of life—their lives, specifically.

For this reason Jesus upon rising from the dead asked his disciples: "Ought not Christ to have suffered these things, and to enter into his glory?" (Luke 24:26, KJV). In short, there was and is a purpose in all that took place in the past, and "beginning at Moses and all the prophets, he expounded unto them in all the scriptures the things concerning himself" (Luke 24:27). And since that divine purpose thus initiated through the Word of God spoken by Moses has been fulfilled in the resurrection, they could turn about-face to walk triumphantly into the future. He becomes for them the seal to God's promise that he shall some glad day be acclaimed King of kings and Lord of lords over all the earth. That understanding alone was enough to turn every one of them around and propel them out into the uttermost parts of the earth as his ambassadors.

Once they were dead in trespasses and sin, all the time drifting along on the stream of this world's idea of living; now Christ has given them life! Perplexed, bewildered, and fearful for their own safety, they now remember his saying: "The works that I do ye shall do also; yea, and greater works than this shall ye do, because I go to my Father" (see John 14:12). The future belongs to him, and to them, because as Jesus said: "Ye shall receive power, after that the Holy Ghost is come upon you: and ye shall be [my] witnesses unto me both in Jerusalem, and in all Judaea, and in Samaria, and unto the uttermost part of the earth" (Acts 1:8, KJV).

And so completely were they turned around that they went everywhere preaching the gospel of God concerning his Son, and the momentum of their words and work goes apace across the face of the whole earth today. His name is passed from mouth to mouth and from generation to generation. Some glad day—may it be soon—at the sounding forth of the name of Jesus, "every knee should bow . . . and every tongue confess that Jesus Christ is Lord, to the glory of God the Father" (Philippians 2:10-11).

Wherefore, shall we not celebrate his resurrection with renewed faith this year? The Grand Purpose of God to call out from all the races of men a people to bear his name is still alive with meaning and great power. The past may be full of tragedy, loss, and despair—enough to make us weep; but it also affords us "the full assurance of understanding" that God's plans are unfailing, that "the path of the just is as the shining light, that shineth more and more [brightly] unto the perfect day" (Proverbs 4:18, KJV).

Indeed, we shall know that we are turned around when we are turned on for him; when "old things are passed away; behold, all things are become new" (2 Corinthians 5:17, KJV); when for the joy that is set before us, we endure our cross (or crosses) and, despising whatever shame men may heap upon us, press forward toward the prize of the high calling of God which reaches us through Christ. For only those whom he turns around can forget the things that are behind since they look toward the dawn of another Day when men will sing a new song, saying:

> Blessing, and honour, and glory, and power
> be unto him that sitteth upon the throne and unto the Lamb
> for ever and ever (Revelation 5:13, KJV).

TELL EVERYONE IT IS TRUE

BILLY GRAHAM

When Dr. W. E. Sangster, England's great Methodist preacher, lay dying with muscular atrophy, he wrote me a letter. In it he said, "All my life I have preached that Jesus Christ is adequate for every crisis. I have but a few days to live, and oh, Billy, Christ is indeed adequate in the hour of death. Tell everyone it is true. Tell them from me that God is wonderfully near his children as they come to the end of life's road."

The day before John Huss was to be burned at the stake, he wrote, "I write this in prison and in chains, expecting tomorrow to receive sentence of death, full of hope in God that I shall not swerve from the truth. I will this day joyfully die."

Is the hope and peace and joy of the resurrection yours today when you contemplate death? I have found that you can tell how a man values life by his estimate of death. Tell me what a man believes about death, and I will tell you what he thinks of life.

Billy Graham is the best-known evangelist of the twentieth century and the most widely heard evangelist in Christian history. Born at the close of World War I, Billy Graham felt the call to preach while a student in Bible school. His contact with the Youth for Christ movement of the 1940s launched his career. His now famous "Los Angeles Campaign" of 1949 gave him national publicity and led to global campaigns of evangelism. A popular radio and television preacher, Graham has written best-selling books, such as *Peace with God* and *Angels.*

Nothing in life is more important than your appointment with destiny and your date with death. Are you certain that you are prepared? David said, "Yea, though I walk through the valley of the shadow of death, I will fear no evil: for thou art with me" (Psalm 23:4, KJV). Our Lord Jesus Christ himself went down into the grave and came forth with the keys of death and hell in his hands.

We think of the cross as being at the very center of Christianity, and it is. And yet apart from the resurrection the cross stands for death, not life. It is possible for us to stand on the wrong side of Easter and look at the cross all our lives and never be redeemed or saved.

No other word in all our vocabulary is more expressive of the message of Jesus Christ than the word "resurrection." In our imagination we see some of the disciples at Calvary watching their Lord die. They saw his broken body taken from the cross. Earlier one of them had betrayed him for thirty pieces of silver. Another had cursed and sworn that he never knew him. Most of them had turned and run for their lives, forsaking him. When he was placed in the tomb and the stone was rolled against it, it seemed that it was the end of all their hopes and dreams.

Then came Easter, and their midnight of despair was turned into a glorious morning. It was the resurrection of all their hopes. Calvary did not tell the whole story. He not only died for our sins, but also the apostle Paul says he was "raised again for our justification" (Romans 4:25, KJV).

Several years ago I was in Bonn, Germany, and I had the privilege of speaking with the venerable post-war chancellor, Konrad Adenauer. We were in his offices in the capitol of the Federal Republic. After we had exchanged greetings and he had poured a cup of coffee for me, he turned to me and said, "Young man, do you believe that Jesus Christ is alive?"

I replied, "Yes, sir, I do."

He said, "So do I. If Jesus Christ is not alive, then I see no hope for the world. It is the fact of the resurrection that gives me hope for the future." And as the aged chancellor spoke those words, his eyes lighted up.

Indeed, this is the only hope of the world at this hour. "If Christ be not risen . . . then . . . your faith is also vain" (1 Corinthians 15:14, KJV). The world, as we well know, is on a collision course. It is heading for trouble. A judgment of such magnitude is being prepared that the human race could not survive if left to itself.

But Christ is alive! And because he is alive, it makes all the difference. In his resurrection, evil has been defeated; love has conquered hate; death has lost its sting; Satan has been defeated; God has accepted the atoning work of his Son on the cross; and all of creation is bursting forth in a new song.

Christ is alive! What tremendous power those words will have if only we will believe! Our faith is so weak. We are such earthbound creatures that it is almost impossible even for the average Christian to believe that Christ is alive. The letter to the Hebrews speaks of "the God of peace, that brought again from the dead our Lord Jesus" (Hebrews 13:20, KJV). That is our God. The early Christians preached it. They believed it. They believed that God had brought Jesus from the dead. They believed that the same power that raised the Lord Jesus from the dead will work in and through us to bring us from our doubts, our darkness, our failure, and even from our death.

As we look at our world today, only a fool can fail to be disturbed by what is happening. Men who have given their lives to scientific investigation are informing us that mankind faces the real threat of nuclear destruction. Environmentalists warn us about the danger of racial suffocation by overpopulation. Sociologists predict an increase in racial frictions and tensions leading to war. The armaments race is proceeding headlong despite the SALT talks. The energy crisis is upon us; our natural resources are running out.

But the resurrection of Jesus Christ tells every true believer that he need not be unduly alarmed. He need not wring his hands and ask, "What shall I do at this hour?" He need not press the panic button. Our concern remains; our social responsibility is still ours to discharge; and it is certain that we shall continue to pray for this earth and its future, but we need not cry in terror as others do.

One of the great bonuses of being a Christian is the great hope that extends beyond the grave into the glory of God's tomorrow. The Bible opens with a tragedy and ends in triumph. In Genesis we see the devastation of sin and death, but in Revelation we see the victory over these forces.

The resurrection of Jesus Christ not only saves man from spiritual death, but it also takes the sting out of physical death for the believer. It robs the grave of its victory. Death is the enemy of mankind; it is something mysterious to be feared, but Christ takes the sting out of it.

Listen to the apostle Paul as he lifts the trumpet of resurrection glory and sounds a note from the heights of immortal ecstasy: "This corruptible must put on incorruption, and this mortal must put on immortality. . . . Then shall be brought to pass the saying that is written, Death is swallowed up in victory" (1 Corinthians 15:53-55), KJV).

A little girl was running toward the cemetery as the darkness of evening began to fall. She passed a friend who asked her if she was not afraid to go through the graveyard at night. "Oh, no," she said, "I'm not afraid. My home is just on the other side!" We Christians are not afraid of the night of death because our heavenly home is "just on the other side."

The resurrection of Christ changed the midnight of bereavement into a sunrise of reunion; it changed the midnight of disappointment into a sunrise of joy; it changed the midnight of fear to a sunrise of peace. That is the reason at Easter I would point you to Jesus Christ who is the same yesterday, today, and forever. All of the disappointment that the disciples experienced came to them because they had failed to accept the fact of the resurrection. I invite you to receive the resurrected Christ, the risen, living Christ today. He can change your life and make you the happiest person in all the world.

Are you suffering from sickness, disappointment, and bereavement? Look for your risen Lord in your garden of disappointment, for "disappointment" is often "his appointment" for you. All your vain hopes and aspirations can be revived when you accept the fact of the resurrection and come into personal contact with the risen Christ.

If you do not know Christ, you have every reason to fear God. You have every reason to fear death. You have every reason to fear the future. But today faith and confidence in a resurrected Christ can change your fear to hope, and your disappointment to joy. Today the risen Christ can live in your heart by the power of the Spirit of God. He can make you a new person if you will surrender to him as Lord and Master and Savior.

At this Easter season let's make the message ring loud and clear like a church bell on Sunday morning, telling the world that its hope lies not in the broken plans and shattered dreams of men, but in the power of the risen Christ. As Dr. Sangster said in his dying moment, "Tell everyone it is true!"

EASTER CHRISTIANS

OSWALD C. J. HOFFMANN

As farmers and townspeople in the Old World walked to church on Easter morning, they were accustomed to greet each other with a ringing shout: "Christ is risen!" Their friends and neighbors shouted in reply, "He is risen, indeed!"

What a great day Easter is, with its dramatic reminder that Christ is alive. Christ has conquered. There is hope for humanity. All of this takes us back a long time.

A few sad-eyed women were picking their way to the tomb in the early morning darkness when the thrill of discovery came with electrifying suddenness. He was not there! A woman wept in the soft light of early morning, her heart crushed over her shattered hopes. He was gone, and she did not know where they had laid him. Then he appeared! People came with leaden hearts and went forth with winged feet to tell the story of what had happened.

That morning God brought all men everywhere under the spell of immortality. What happened on Easter morning can bring

---

Oswald C. J. Hoffmann was born in Snyder, Nebraska, and received his education at the University of Minnesota and Concordia Seminary. He is an ordained minister of the Lutheran Church, Missouri Synod. In 1955 he succeeded the late Dr. Walter A. Maier as preacher on the "Lutheran Hour." He has served on the councils of the Berlin and Minneapolis congresses on evangelism. In addition to his worldwide radio preaching, he is a writer and film producer.

---

perpetual morning to your life, if you will join St. Peter in his glorious recollection of what happened to him that morning. His words are recorded in the first epistle of Peter, chapter 1, verse 3:

"Thank God, the God and Father of our Lord Jesus Christ, that in his great mercy we men have been born again into a life full of hope, through Christ's rising again from the dead!" (J.B. Phillips).

"The Lord is risen indeed, and hath appeared unto Simon," was the whisper passed from mouth to mouth among the astonished disciples on the first Easter morning. They were astonished because they had not really expected him to fulfill his promise that he would rise again. Yet here he was, after being crucified and laid in a grave, now alive and walking among living men. First one and then another, then groups of his friends, and, finally, large bodies of people were privileged to see the Conqueror of the grave, to listen to him, to speak with him, to touch him, to eat with him, as a convincing testimony that Calvary was not the end. It was just the beginning!

The resurrection of Jesus Christ is the fundamental fact which satisfies Christians of the truth of the religion of Jesus Christ. It assures them that the forgiveness of God is real and that their own resurrection to life everlasting is not just a probability but an actuality. When the apostles went forth after his ascension into heaven to convert the world to his gospel, what did they preach? Any child who has read the Acts of the Apostles knows the answer: they preached the resurrection of Jesus Christ.

"The Lord is risen indeed, and hath appeared to Simon" (Luke 24:34, KJV). What did Simon have to say about that? This is what he said: "Thank God, the God and Father of our Lord Jesus Christ, that in his great mercy we have been born again into a life full of hope, through Christ's rising again from the dead!" (1 Peter 1:3, J.B. Phillips).

People talk today as if the apostles who proclaimed the resurrection came from an unscientific past when people would believe anything. Too bad, they say, that Christianity could not be tested by our doubting, clear-headed, scientific methods. The disciples and the common people of our Lord's time are pictured by these advanced thinkers as people pathetically eager to be fooled, or intent on fooling themselves.

The fact is that the apostles had to contend in the first Christian century with smothering unbelief. In the face of sheer disdain toward the story of a physical resurrection, they conceded nothing. They went right ahead telling the story over and over again. They were men who had seen and could not be dissuaded from telling what they had seen. The historian of the Acts of the Apostles tells us what they preached: "With great power gave the apostles witness of the resurrection of the Lord Jesus" (Acts 4:33, KJV).

The apostles would have welcomed the appointment of an investigative committee to examine their claims. They had nothing to lose from investigation and everything to gain by the most thorough and searching inquiry. They were sure of their facts. As a consequence they boldly asserted what they knew to be true, even in the face of the keenest, bitterest, and most contemptuous incredulity.

They had staked their lives on the fact of the resurrection of Christ. We may be sure that they looked hard at it again and again, as men will whose very existence depends on a certain fact. The more they looked, the more they believed, and the more they knew. In the conviction of faith they acquired a confidence more unshakable than any that has ever been founded upon verified scientific hypothesis.

Verified scientific hypothesis has failed before, and it will fail again. Robert Oppenheimer has stated that basic conceptions regarding the organization of the universe will have to be radically revised as the result of studies in nuclear physics during this last decade. It may take another generation, he said, before someone comes forward with a unifying principle such as Max Planck's formulation which dominated scientific thinking up to 1950.

But the resurrection stands unshaken in lonely grandeur, a pillar of faith unmoved by the swirling tides of time. You can't deny it and still be a convinced Christian. You can't push it into the background and still share in the assurance that has marked Christian faith since the year one of the Christian era. Every Christian, every person alive, has a great stake in the resurrection. It is the guarantee of God's mercy, by which alone men can be born again into the living hope of which St. Peter speaks. The philosopher Jean Paul Richter wrote: "I have gazed into the gulf beyond and cried, 'Father, where art Thou?' But no answer came save the storm. We are orphans, you and I. Every soul in this corpse-trench of the universe is utterly alone." That's what a philosopher says when he looks into the grave. But listen to what God has to say. He speaks in the thunderous tones of action. The stone has been rolled away, and the Lord Christ has risen from the dead to become the pioneer of those who sleep in the grave.

We are not alone. He is risen. From the tomb, he walks back into our lives. Death has not changed him. His love has not ended. His compassion has not folded up. His forgiveness has not shriveled away. He knows each of us as he knew Mary by her sadness, Peter by his faults, Thomas by his doubts.

Thank God, there is something for each of us in the resurrection of Jesus Christ. By the mercy of God there is something of courage, of strength, of hope for us. The resurrection is God's answer to man's failure—to our failure, whatever it may be.

Are you weighted down with any care, any worry, any sorrow? Are you crushed and defeated by a certain weakness you have tried to overcome, without success? Has the constant pounding of life knocked all the hope out of you? Cast all these cares, these worries, these sorrows, these frustrations aside. Christ the Lord is risen today! "Thank God, the God and Father of our Lord Jesus Christ, that in his great mercy we have been born again into a life full of hope, through Christ's rising again from the dead!" (1 Peter 1:3, J.B. Phillips).

If faith in Christ were just a sentiment, it would last just for a day. But the resurrection is a fact. Because it is a fact, the mercy of God is a fact, too. The forgiving mercy of God is a fact you can depend upon, to be born again to a new life full of hope. This is a faith good for sunshiny days, and for rainy, foggy days as well, when vision is obscured and the heart is heavy.

"Because I live," said Christ, "you will live also" (John 14:19*b*).

"I live," said St. Paul, "yet not I, but Christ liveth in me" (Galatians 2:20, KJV).

This is year-round religion, the kind that belongs to a real Easter Christian. An Easter Christian, you see, is not one who comes to church on Easter Sunday and then isn't seen again until next year at Easter time. He is the kind of man who moves as the living Christ moves in and with him. He knows Christ. He believes in Christ. He loves Christ. He obeys Christ. He follows Christ. He lives for Christ. In other words, he lives the life full of hope, described by St. Peter: "Thank God, the God and Father of our Lord Jesus Christ, that in his great mercy we have been born again into a life full of hope, through Christ's rising again from the dead!" (1 Peter 1:3, J.B. Phillips).

On Good Friday, the world said "no." On Easter Sunday, God said "yes." In his mercy he says "yes" to you today.

Say "yes" to him at this Eastertide. Be born again, into a new life, full of hope, by his rising from the dead!

I, PILATE

HAROLD F. LEESTMA

My name is Pontius Pilate. I have come back to
the earth to tell you my story.
    I was faced with the supreme test of my life
      and I failed.
    I was in charge of a large area of Palestine,
representing the Roman government. I had
worked in that area for ten years. The emperor,
Tiberius Caesar, was pleased with my work.
I built myself a beautiful palace. I got along
with the Jewish people even though I detested
their legalistic religion.
    You think I was a cruel,
      hardhearted Roman judge.
    Please understand I fought a battle within my soul.
    I had an inner struggle similar to yours.
This is how it happened . . .
A lot of hostility had arisen against a man

Harold F. Leestma, a native of Grand Rapids, Michigan, received his education from Hope College and Western Theological Seminary. He served pastorates in Michigan and Indiana before entering a ministry as co-pastor of the Garden Grove Community Church, California. An ordained minister of the Reformed Church of America, Leestma has published several booklets on the Christian life.

---

named Jesus. Some activists in that anti-Jesus
movement came during the night to my palace.
They would not step inside.
They sent a messenger and told me to
come out to them.
I walked to the balcony where I could see,
and it was quite a crowd.
They had with them a man.
They were treating him roughly and were
shouting things I couldn't understand.
And then they said to me,
"We have a prisoner. We want you to
judge him."
I asked,
"What accusation do you have against this man?"
They replied,
"If we didn't have an accusation, we
wouldn't have brought him to you."
I said to them,
"Take him and try him according to your laws."
But then I heard their answer,
"No."
"Why not?"
"According to our laws,
we cannot put a man to death."
That was it. They wanted this man's life.
I ordered them to bring the man up. He stood
before me and before the crowd. I looked into his face.
I thought I would see hostility or hatred,
or hear whimpering and whining.
No! There was calmness.
I saw him gaze out at the crowd with compassion.
I had looked into the faces of many prisoners
before but never one like this. So I asked
him some questions. Then I said to the people,
"I find no fault in this man. None at all!"
Somehow they wouldn't accept that. It was so
noisy that one of their leaders, Caiaphas, climbed
the steps toward my balcony.He held his robe
tightly about him so he wouldn't defile himself. He said,

"This man is an insurrectionist. He's a troublemaker."

I said,

"Caiaphas, I'd like to have a lot more men like him in my province."

Then I turned to the man and said,

"They tell me you claim to be a king. Is this true? You're a king?"

Since I spoke it in contempt, he never answered, and I knew why. I knew that if I leveled with him, he would level with me. I continued,

"My security men say that when you entered the city gate a few days ago, the people and children waved palm branches and called you a king. Is that true?"

He replied,

"Yes, I am a King."

"But my kingdom," he explained, "is not of this world." We talked some more, and once again I turned to the crowd:

"I find no fault in him at all. Take him and try him according to your laws."

But Caiaphas wouldn't give up. He kept shouting at me, and I heard him mention "Galilee." I said,

"Did you say 'Galilee'?"

He said, "Yes."

I asked,

"Do you mean this man is from Galilee?"

"Yes, yes."

"My jurisdiction," I told Caiaphas, "does not include Galilee. That belongs to Herod, and it so happens he is in Jerusalem tonight, staying at his palace."

I turned to my guard: "Take this man to Herod." I swung around and went into my room, but somehow I knew I was not through with him. I knew I'd face him again.

Looking out my window, I watched the crowd break up. My soldiers were there, and they were rough with this man. My heart went out to

him. I tried to eat, to drink. I couldn't.
My mind reeled with the thought of the Person I had just met. I knew he was a noted teacher. My wife, Claudia, had heard him a few times.

One day she had come home and said,

"This man even performs miracles."

This was too much for me, but some of his teaching about justice and truth and love had impressed me.

It was only a short time until I heard the crowd return. They had the prisoner with them. Herod, that fox, was sending him back to me. Suddenly I had an idea. I said to the guard,

"Go to the inner dungeon and bring up Barabbas."

"Barabbas, sir?"

"Yes, Barabbas."

And soon I had the two men standing there together.

Barabbas, the rebel, the murderer,
Jesus, the Teacher, the Healer, the Helper.

I called the people together and said,

"Which of these two shall I set free?
Barabbas, the insurgent, the killer, or
Jesus, who is called Christ?"

I couldn't believe what I heard. They shouted,

"Barabbas, Barabbas! Release Barabbas!"

I gave an order to my guard:

"Untie Barabbas."

I said to him,

"You're free."

As he passed me to leave, he looked at me and spat on me. One of my guards struck him to the floor. I said,

"Leave him alone."

Barabbas got to his feet, bewildered, and turned to Jesus.

Jesus was looking at him with a love I had
never seen on anyone's face.

Barabbas went out into the night.
I called a recess and went into my room. I paced the floor.

Suddenly I heard a scream behind me. I turned, drawing my dagger. Claudia, my wife, ran into the room and threw her arms around me and said,

"Pontius, I've had a terrible dream."

I said,

"Claudia, forget about dreams. I've got important things to think about." Then,

"Oh, Claudia, what shall I do with Jesus? Help me!"

She said,

"Have nothing to do with this good man."

I stepped out again to the balcony. I planned to say,

"I've examined this man. He is a just man, a good man. I will protect him with the legions of Rome.

"This man is free!"

Then I thought about my position in the government and my standing with the people. I thought about my finances. I compromised.

"I'll have him whipped and then release him," I decided. I ordered a guard to take the leather thongs with the sharp pieces of metal and to give him forty stripes, save one. I noticed that my soldiers were having a little fun.

They had made a crown of thorns
and put it on his head.
The blood was running down his face.
They had to hold him up.
I should have stopped their horseplay,
but I didn't.
I, Pontius Pilate, looked again, and knew
I had to make a decision.
"What shall I do with Jesus, who is called
Christ?"
I called on the gods. I was determined to
say of this man,
"Truly he is the Son of God."
But the words didn't come . . .
That's why I have come back to tell you about it.
I made the wrong decision.

I've carried a remorse that nothing can heal.
I've come to tell you:
don't blame your environment;
don't blame circumstances;
don't blame teachers, parents, preachers.
You face Jesus Christ personally
and make the right decision.
I was just ready to do it, but something overcame me. Instead, I turned to an aide and said,
"Get a basin of water."
He set the basin on the balcony, and I washed my hands.
I shouted to the crowd,
"See, I am innocent of the blood of this just man."
Now I must go. But what about you?
You know so much more about him than I did.
You have a book called the Bible.
It tells all about this man.
You have the witness of the Christian church through the centuries.
You can see the people who have made the wrong decision and the destructive forces at work in their lives.
You have all around you the lives of those who have made the right decision and have called him Savior and Lord.
You can see in their lives pardon, peace, power,
and eternal life.
This is your life's most important decision:
What will you do with Jesus, who is called Christ?
What will you do with him?
Farewell.

EASTER'S PRELUDE

DOUGLAS N. MOFFAT

Christians have always associated Christ's victory over death with Easter morning. Customarily we think of the early morning discovery of the open tomb as the first sign that Christ had had a decisive victory over the forces of evil. Certainly it was on Easter morning that his victory became gloriously apparent. But actually the first real sign of Christ's victory over sin and death came not on Easter morning but at the darkest hour of the crucifixion. His last words at Calvary, "Father, into Thy hands I commend my spirit," were but the prelude to the angels' first words at Easter. They remind us that in the darkest hour of history Christ was still in control. Although he was nailed to a cross and his life had ebbed away, he retained the power to deliver his life into the hands of God and not into the hands of the enemy. It was at this very point that Easter's resurrection became a certainty.

This prelude to Easter has three very important truths to teach us. First, divine light is always provided in the midst of darkness. When Jesus cried, "It is finished" and commended his life into the

---

Douglas N. Moffat graduated from Sir George Williams University in Montreal and received his B.D. from McMaster Divinity College in Hamilton, Ontario. He was ordained by the Baptist Convention of Ontario and Quebec in 1962. He presently serves as Senior Pastor of the Braemar Baptist Church, Edmonton, Alberta. He has served actively in the Baptist Conventions of Canada, as well as pastoring Baptist churches in the Atlantic provinces.

hands of the Father, it became apparent to everyone watching his suffering form that the excruciating ordeal was over. For his detractors this was the end of an insurrectionist, a charlatan, a disturber of the peace. For the little band that followed him it was the unbelievable death of their Master. He had been terribly misunderstood and unjustly put to death. But for Christ it was "Mission Completed"—the absolute fulfilling of the will of the Father. He had done all that the Father had asked him to do. If only the light of that truth had dawned upon the disciples as they stood watching him! Here was the divine light penetrating the darkness of Calvary, but they did not perceive it. It dawned upon them only on Easter morning.

There is a town in the extreme north of Norway where on January 18 each year all the people climb a hill in order that they may see the sun rise after many weeks of perpetual night. All they see on that first morning is a glimmering rim of light. For them it is enough. They know that spring will come. And so at Calvary, God provided a thin line of dawning light amid history's darkest hour. It was the Savior's triumphant affirmation that his life was being delivered into the hands of our all-powerful God. If in the darkness of that hour there could be light, how dare any of us deny the light of his presence in our dark hours? When the way seems gloomy and the horizon black, commend your life into the hands of your heavenly Father. This exercise of your faith and trust will become the prelude to new blessings. Of that you can be confident. God is waiting to bring the light of Easter morning into your life in a new dawning.

It was in that spirit that a group of French resistance workers in Nazi-occupied France wrote this creed on a bridge abutment before they gave their lives in the struggle for freedom. "We believe in the dawn though the night be dark." It is the Christ of the resurrection morning that can give each one of us that same indomitable spirit for the dark experiences of life, if only we will commend our lives into his care and keeping.

This prelude to Easter has a second important truth to teach us. Not only is divine light provided in the midst of darkness, but divine grace is also provided in the midst of sin. To his little band of followers the cross of Christ looked like the victory of evil over good. Their sensibilities had been violated by an outrage of injustice, their hearts paralyzed by anxiety and fear, their spirits broken by hopeless despair. The very air hung heavy with sinister and evil foreboding.

And yet even in the vortex of Satan's evil schemes, the grace of God was at work. As the Savior's detractors flung their epithets in his blood-stained face and as the angry mob ridiculed him, the quiet voice of Jesus shook the foundation of hell and thwarted the purposes of Satan with these grace-filled words, "Father, forgive them." But alas! this work of grace in the midst of such evil passed unknown in that awful hour. His disciples did not understand that this poignant prayer was the prelude to the full atoning work of Jesus which burst forth in all its glory when Jesus walked out of the open tomb.

The story is told that, when Wellington defeated Napoleon at Waterloo, the message was flashed by signal code from a ship still out at sea to a coastal lookout on the English shoreline. Only half of the message was relayed when fog closed in. The half message was transmitted to London: "Wellington defeated." Only later, when the fog cleared, was the mistake discovered. The whole message read: "Wellington defeated the enemy." In like manner the oppressive sense of sin at Calvary obscured Christ's victory in a battle that so many thought he had lost when he had actually won. There is a powerful lesson here. Evil need never defeat us, if, in the midst of it, we commit our lives into the Father's care and keeping. In the midst of sin there is the grace of Christ, and his grace is greater. Think of the Scriptures that point to that fact, "Where sin abounded, grace did much more abound" (Romans 5:20, KJV); "If God be for us, who can be against us?" (Romans 8:31, KJV).

The world may see defeat in many of life's situations, but for the Christian it is only half of the message. There is no better example of this than the dying thief. Like Christ he, too, looked finished. But in the midst of his sin and shame, the thief became aware of the grace of Christ beside him. Christ was dying, and yet with the amazing insight of newborn faith the thief could see his suffering as but the prelude to a greater victory. Thus he asked the Master to remember him when he entered his kingdom, and the Master gave him his glad assurance. Nowhere in all the Scripture is there an example of abounding grace more sublimely demonstrated.

Do you feel your life is a loss or so badly tainted with defeat and failure, sin and shame, that a new beginning is impossible? If you do, you are wrong. In the midst of his sin the thief reached out to Christ. So can you. If you do, the Christ of Easter morning will break your bonds and set you free.

The prelude to Easter has a third very important truth to teach us. Not only is divine light provided in the midst of darkness, divine grace provided in the midst of sin, but divine hope is also provided in the midst of despair. No Christian should ever lose sight of one axiom: God always has the last word, and that final word has a way of altering things. Christ's final word thwarted Satan's intended victory. The Savior ended up in the hands of God, not in the hands of the enemy, and that fact changed everything. Because of that final word at Calvary, the cross, man's symbol of sin, death, and defeat became God's symbol of grace, life, and victory so that now we sing, "In the cross of Christ I glory, towering o'er the wrecks of time." If God could so transform the cross, is there any circumstance in your life he cannot transform if you give him the chance to speak his final word? He can bring peace out of pain, joy out of sorrow, wisdom out of failure, love out of hate, hope out of despair.

Do you recall the words of Joseph to his brothers whom he had encountered years after they had tried to take his life? Joseph was now the second in command in Egypt. He was the economic savior of his day. The tables were reversed. The brothers were now in Joseph's power, but he had a far different view of events than they did. He explained to them, "You meant evil against me; but God meant it for good, to bring it about that many people should be kept alive as they are today" (Genesis 50:20). This dramatic change of events and Joseph's magnanimous spirit are explained by one simple thing. Joseph allowed God to have the last word.

There is a mission station in Japan whose meeting house was constructed out of the stones which had been thrown at the local Christians. The stones of adversity became building blocks in the kingdom because God had the last word. History seems to be flinging a great many stones in the pathway of man's progress. There is a pall of despair hanging over the preachments of so many doomsday prophets in contemporary life. The flash points of war are continually close to ignition. The glut of consumption, the blight of pollution, and the frenzied quest for more energy to consume and pollute even more have plunged man into a spiral of retrogression. We despair of the future, but there is hope! God is the Lord of history, working out his purposes in the affairs of men. God will have the last word. He shall consummate history, and with the coming of his kingdom a new day will dawn, more splendid and glorious than the dawning of Easter morning. Jesus summons us to live with resilience by the inspiration of that hope.

Here then are the three lessons which the prelude to Easter teach us and which are worth learning well. Divine light is always provided in the midst of darkness. Divine grace is always provided in the midst of sin. Divine hope is always provided in the midst of despair. Easter makes this very clear. Christ rose victorious from the grave, but the prelude to that great symphony was sounded at Calvary and because it was, you and I can face darkness, sin, and despair and know there is an answer; it is Jesus Christ himself. He promises his victories to you as you give your life to him in faith and trust.

UNSENTIMENTAL JESUS

JOEL NEDERHOOD

One of the reasons many students hesitate to follow Jesus Christ is that the popular picture of Jesus seems so out of place in our modern, revolutionary times. What do you think about when you think about Jesus? Well, I wouldn't be surprised if you think about stained-glass windows, magnificent churches, and sentimental hymns. But that kind of a Jesus just doesn't fit in a world like ours.

What a tragedy that men have turned their backs on Jesus Christ! The combined efforts of the ages have succeeded in making him a figure so exalted that there seems no place at all for him in our bitter, suffering world. It is tragic, because a close examination of the real person, Jesus Christ of Nazareth, discloses that he fits into our world very well. For there is no sorrow like his sorrow.

If you think that Jesus doesn't fit into our world, you should listen to the way he is described in the only real record we have of him. That record is found in the Bible. Although there were great high points in Jesus' life, when his earthly ministry was over, mankind

---

Joel H. Nederhood received his education from Calvin College and Calvin Seminary, Grand Rapids, Michigan. He received his Th.D. degree from the Free University of Amsterdam. Ordained to the ministry by the Christian Reformed Church, Dr. Nederhood has served as speaker and director of the "Back to God" radio program. His writing abilities have led him to the editorship of *Today,* a Chicago publication, and to the authorship of books, such as *God Is Too Much, The Holy Triumph,* and others.

---

took Jesus Christ and put him out like a man squashes a cigarette butt with his heel. Jesus became a nobody, a zero, a nothing, at the end of his earthly ministry.

The Jesus of the stained-glass windows and all the other beautiful trappings we have now associated with his worship is the product of what men have done with him after he died and rose again and ascended into heaven. But in our world it is necessary to remind ourselves that it wasn't this way with Jesus all the time. Jesus went through the fires of deepest affliction and pain on behalf of his people, and that was no accident. It was an integral part of what Jesus lived and died to do. He came into this world to walk the lowest road a man has ever walked, the road that skirts the fringes of damnation and then leads into the very flames of hell.

In the Old Testament section of the Bible, the prophet Isaiah foretold how it would be with Jesus. This is what he said in chapter 53 of his book: "He was despised and rejected by men; a man of sorrows, and acquainted with grief; and as one from whom men hide their faces he was despised, and we esteemed him not" (v. 3). This whole chapter in the book of Isaiah points forward to the coming Messiah of Israel. I don't suppose Isaiah understood exactly what he was saying when he wrote these words under the inspiration of the Holy Spirit. But there it is, shocking as blood spattered on the sidewalk: Jesus Christ, the unique Son of God, became the great discarded man, so despised and abandoned that nobody would think of giving him a second glance.

The old prophet Isaiah's vision of what Jesus was going to go through came true. When you read the Gospels in the New Testament, you find at the end of each of them the record of Jesus' capture, his trial by the religious leaders, his appearance before representatives of the Roman government, and his crucifixion. Just to give you a flavor of what happened, let me refer to certain sentences from the last chapters of Matthew.

Jesus appeared before the religious leaders of his nation. The high priest commanded him point-blank, "I adjure you by the living God, tell us if you are the Christ, the Son of God" (Matthew 26:63). Jesus said that he was. The religious leaders immediately condemned him for blasphemy and concluded that Jesus deserved death. Because they did not have the legal authority to carry out the death sentence, they had to bring him before Pilate, the Roman governor.

Pilate heard their accusations, and then he asked Jesus to defend himself. Pilate was somewhat uneasy. He was not sure that Jesus was guilty of a crime that deserved death, and his wife had warned him that he should not harm Jesus. So he tried to squirm out of the necessity of crucifying Jesus. Matthew explains what Pilate tried to do this way: "Now at the feast the governor was accustomed to release for the crowd any one prisoner whom they wanted. And they had then a notorious prisoner, called Barabbas. . . . Pilate said to them, 'Whom do you want me to release for you, Barabbas or Jesus who is called Christ?'" The people chose Barabbas. "Pilate said to them, 'Then what shall I do with Jesus who is called Christ?' They all said, 'Let him be crucified'" (Matthew 27:15-22).

After this happened, the Roman governor turned Jesus over to rough Roman soldiers so that he could become their plaything for a little while before he was crucified. They mocked him by throwing one of their old, worn-out army blankets over his shoulders, pushing an old walking stick into his hand, pressing a crown of thorns upon his head, and then shouting at him and taunting him. The soldiers demonstrated that all of Jesus' rights had been stripped away. He just didn't count anymore. He was man's great discarded man, ejected from the human race.

The Bible spares nothing to make this point absolutely clear: Jesus was forcibly cut off from ordinary human society. When we review the events surrounding Jesus' trial and crucifixion, we observe that every class of people was involved in this rejection. The religious leaders of the people led the way, and this is a chilling warning for all religious leaders today. In the rejection of the Messiah on the part of the very leaders who claimed to be leading the people to the Messiah, we see just how mistaken religious experts can be. But the common people joined in the rejection, too, for it was their shouts that finally sent Jesus to the cross. The state was also involved in this rejection, for Pilate represented the mighty Roman empire when he allowed Jesus' unjust condemnation to be carried out. Even Jesus' own disciples turned away from him and left him to suffer alone. Though Jesus' followers did not reject him with the same vicious malice others demonstrated, it was one of Jesus' inner circle, Judas, who betrayed him. All of this combines to make Jesus the man who became no man for the sake of all humanity.

Why did it have to be this way? What is God telling us here, as we observe the utter rejection of his only Son? You really cannot understand what is happening in all of this until you go back into the

Old Testament history and read the record of a scapegoat.

In Leviticus 16, you read how the high priest of the people of Israel had to conduct certain ceremonies in order to take away the people's sin. Many of these ceremonies were conducted within the tabernacle. But after certain tabernacle ceremonies had been completed, something very interesting happened. There was a goat waiting outside as the priest came out. This is what we read: "And when he has made an end of atoning for the holy place and the tent of meeting and the altar, he shall present the live goat; and Aaron shall lay both his hands upon the head of the live goat, and confess over him all the iniquities of the people of Israel, and all their transgressions, all their sins; and he shall put them upon the head of the goat, and send him away into the wilderness by the hand of a man who is in readiness. The goat shall bear all their iniquities upon him to a solitary land; and he shall let the goat go in the wilderness" (vv. 20-22).

All the sins of the people of Israel were laid on that goat, and then the goat was led away into a solitary place. He was cut off from any association with the people. And that is what was happening in the great rejection of Jesus, too. The people who participated in that rejection of Jesus did not know what they were doing. But God knew what they were doing, and Jesus knew what they were doing, and we can know what they were doing. Jesus Christ had voluntarily become the great sin bearer. We read in 2 Corinthians 5:21 that "for our sake he made him to be sin who knew no sin, so that in him we might become the righteousness of God." Jesus, in his great love for man, became the scapegoat, not just for the sins of a single nation, but for the sins of all people of all races who believe on him. He became the great sin bearer, and all the sins of the world were spoken over his head. And because he was the scapegoat, he had to be led away to a solitary place and cut off from the human race.

Because he willingly identified himself totally with sin, it had to be this way. All this highlights the fact that Jesus' suffering and his eventual death were not just private tragedies or personal catastrophes. As Jesus went through all that we have been talking about, God was busy working a great work of salvation for sinful people.

You will simply miss the point of Jesus' life and death and final resurrection unless you see that. There is essentially only one problem that we are all working with and trying to solve, and that is the problem of sin. I don't mean to be simplistic here, but there are times when we have to reduce to its lowest common denominator all that we fight against and all that frustrates us and makes us bitter. Our personal problems, our national problems, and the international problems that convulse our world are all because we lie under a curse. Man is selfish, narrow, small, murderous, and hateful. All of this is because of sin. Somehow the great problem of human sin must be solved before there is any hope for restoration and happiness.

After you have read the whole Bible and you have let its message crash down over your head and humble you, you finally see that the great message of the Old and New Testaments is that man is sinful, but God has sent his Son into the world to be the sin bearer. And Jesus went all the way with that sin, even to the point where his fellowmen shook their heads and turned their eyes away from the utter humiliation he experienced. He hurled himself, with all the precious beauty of his perfect human and divine person, into the very jaws of hell and willingly bore man's every insult and bitter scorn in order that something could happen to right the ugly wrongs that have plagued the human race since the fall of man into sin.

When we look at this Jesus, he fits right into the kind of world we are living in today. The romanticized Jesus, the Jesus of the stained-glass windows, is out of place. The stained-glass window Jesus doesn't fit very well into the ghetto where people experience the cutting edge of poverty and the devastating results of discrimination. The stained-glass window Jesus doesn't fit into the steaming cities filled with crippled, starving people. He doesn't fit into the ambiguity and horror of Vietnam and the Middle East. But the real Jesus you find in the Bible does. He can come and stand right next to anybody and everybody, and when he does, we discover that he is our brother. If we are down, torn by circumstances of life, we discover that Jesus Christ, too, "was despised and rejected by men" (Isaiah 53:3).

The real Jesus fits right into our terrifying world because he experienced the same terror you do when your fellowmen turn on you. But he fits in for another reason, too. Jesus alone provides a solution to our greatest problem. His suffering was different from ours. Our suffering is so often futile, but his accomplished something.

Jesus fits into our world perfectly. He fits into your life because, if you believe in him, he will take your sins away. Don't you think you had better stop listening to all the sentimental things people say about Jesus and start looking at the real Jesus—the one the Bible describes so fully? When you do that, you will find a Savior.

UNDERSTANDING CALVARY

HAROLD JOHN OCKENGA

I have a wonderful text. It opens up the counsels of the Trinity, the mysteries of redemption, and the glories of heaven. Would I had the tongue of an angel to declare it! It is the truth of redemption by the cross. It, not the virgin birth, not the miracles of Christ, not the Second Coming of the Lord, is the very center of the Christian message (1 Corinthians 1:23; 2:2).

My text is: "And they understood none of these things; and this saying was hid from them, neither knew they the things which were spoken" (Luke 18:34, KJV).

Calvary was plainly foretold by Jesus, repeatedly and understandably. Yet the apostles did not grasp what he said. A strange incomprehensibility rested upon these disciples so that they could not understand plain language. Luke 9:31 says of Moses and Elias, "Who appeared in glory, and spake of his decease which he should accomplish at Jerusalem"; Luke 9:51 says, "When the time was come that he should be received up, he stedfastly set his face to go to

---

Harold John Ockenga served for thirty-two years as pastor of Park Street Church, Boston, and was the first president of the National Association of Evangelicals. He serves as president of the board of *Christianity Today* and is actively associated with the Billy Graham Evangelistic Association. After resigning his pastorate, Ockenga became president of Gordon College and Gordon-Conwell Theological Seminary, both located near Boston. He has authored more than a dozen books and is a frequent contributor to evangelical periodicals.

Jerusalem"; and now we have this plain statement of Luke 18:31-34. Matthew is just as plain in his record of the statements of Jesus concerning the inevitability of Calvary (Matthew 16:21; 17:12*b*; 17:22, 23; 20:18, 19). In spite of these clear statements, the disciples did not understand.

Calvary was foreseen and foretold by the prophets. Every sacrifice according to the law looked forward to this; Psalm 22 and Psalm 69 described the sufferings of the Messiah; Isaiah 52:12 to 53:11 delineated these sufferings; Daniel 9:26 and Zechariah 13:6-7 referred to it; yet no one in the time of Jesus understood the Old Testament prophecies concerning the suffering servant in the Messianic sense. Only at a later time did some of the Jewish rabbis teach that there would be a suffering Messiah (Messiah ben Joseph) and a triumphant Messiah (Messiah ben Judah). Not even the prophets themselves understood what they wrote (1 Peter 1:10).

Our text says that the meaning of Calvary was hidden from the apostles. Did God deliberately hide it from them? If so, why? It was hidden from them for several reasons: First, that God's eternal plan might be fulfilled, namely, to make Christ Jesus our substitute in the satisfaction of the law. From eternity God the Father decreed the death of Jesus on the cross. He was the lamb slain from before the foundation of the world. Second, it was hidden that wicked men might kill the Prince of Life. Peter declared that if they had known the identity of Jesus, they would not have crucified the Lord of glory. Their decision was an independent one, but it was embraced in the plan of God. Third, it was hidden from them that God might turn their evil actions to good. God's love matched man's sin. The fall of the Jews was to be the riches of the nations, and it was embraced for this purpose.

It is strange about our capacity to understand. This capacity changes with different ages. What you could not grasp as a child, or as a youth, you now can understand. At one time you did not understand the value of music and you refused to have any part of it, but now you understand and regret your decision. At one time you did not understand the value of financial thrift and resultant security; now you understand and regret your prodigality of youth. Once you did not understand fidelity in human relationships, but now you understand, possibly with deep regret.

The understanding of Calvary was granted to the apostles through the post-resurrection interpretation by Christ and through

Pentecost. As the resurrected Christ explained the necessity of his sufferings from the Law, the Psalms, and the Prophets, their eyes were opened and their hearts burned within them. When the Holy Ghost came upon them at Pentecost and they were guided into the fullness of truth, all the strands of truth fell together into an harmonious whole. From that time on, the apostles were in unanimous agreement of the necessity of the death and resurrection of Christ which constituted the gospel.

Calvary can be understood and known only by regenerate persons (1 Corinthians 2:14). Because of this, men do not understand Calvary today. For God to die on a cross seems ridiculous to the unregenerate. Natural reason cannot comprehend this. The human mind must be renewed in regeneration by the Holy Spirit if it is to understand Calvary. Students who are filled with questions concerning the goodness of God, predestination and freedom, the problem of human suffering, the dual nature of Christ, and the understanding of the Trinity find that when their central question is answered, many of their other questions disappear. In my own Christian counseling I listen to the problem or the question that an inquirer has, and then I turn the conversation to Calvary and the knowledge of salvation. Once this question is settled, it is easy to face other questions. When a person is regenerate, the mystery is no longer hidden but open.

Calvary must be understood in the framework of theology. There is a divine reason for the cross.

Wisdom dictated that justice and mercy, holiness and goodness should all be satisfied, and it found a way for them to meet in the cross (Psalm 85:10). There was no other way for such reconciliation, atonement, and mediation than Calvary. If there had been, Jesus' prayer in Gethsemane, "If it be possible, let this cup pass from me," would have been answered by the removal of Calvary. When Jesus cried, "It is finished," all the demands of the attributes of God which had been affected by sin were satisfied.

Another way to understand the cross is by experience. This experience is three-fold. First, the cross is the way of salvation. It is the only way to come to God, the only means of salvation, the only bridge from sinful man to holy God. It is the essence of the gospel which is presented throughout the entire Bible.

The second way of experiencing the cross is for sanctification or victory of Christian life. The believer accepts the cross as the means of his dying to the old man. He takes his position with Christ as crucified to the old nature and the motions of sin. By faith he reckons himself to be dead. Once the believer so accepts the cross, he may then be united with Christ in resurrection life. By the Spirit he is quickened and seated with Christ in heavenly places. Thus, the resurrected, glorified, reigning Christ may release the Spirit in the life of the crucified and resurrected believer, producing all the fruit of the Spirit which makes the believer like unto Christ.

The third meaning of the cross in Christian experience is as a way of service or of living. The principle was set down by the Lord Jesus when he said, "Except a corn of wheat fall to the ground and die, it abideth alone, but if it die, it bringeth forth much fruit" (John 12:24, KJV). The cross must become a constant way of life. The believer must voluntarily accept his position of self-denial, sacrifice, and service for Christ's sake. Insofar as he does this, he shall find it.

Though there is much that the believer understands about Calvary, there is much he will never understand. Christians will never know the depths of suffering which Christ Jesus endured on the cross. We know that he tasted death (Hebrews 2:14), and what a death it was! We know that he endured the curse of the broken law (Galatians 3:13) and that that curse will never rest upon the believer. We know that he carried the wrath of God which was holiness in motion against the sin of humanity held back and dammed up through the ages and then released to overwhelm Christ Jesus on the cross (Romans 3:25-26). It was this that overwhelmed Christ and broke his heart.

We can never know the full mystery of what occurred on Calvary. How did God die on the cross? How did he take death into himself? If he had not done these things, how could the atonement have been made effective for the believers? When will the human mind ever understand this, and where shall we ever find language to express this?

But let's ask these same disciples who did not understand when Jesus told them of Calvary what they now understand about it.

How about you, Peter? What do you understand about Calvary?

"I saw them take him away from Caiaphas's hall after I was offended because he did not accept my defense of him by force. It seems incredible, impossible that I did not stand with him in that hour, but I did not understand. But now I know. I know that it was the Prince of Life they crucified. I know that Christ has once suffered for sin, the just for the unjust, that he might bring us to God, being put to death in the flesh but quickened by the Spirit. I know that Calvary was the means to life."

And how about you, John? You were very close to Christ. What do you think of Calvary now?

"I stood with Jesus through it all: through the trial in Caiaphas's hall, through the suffering on Golgotha and through the agony of the cross. It was all so dark and confusing that I did not understand. Then, on the resurrection day, when he appeared to us and explained it, saying that it behooved Christ to suffer and rise from the dead the third day, that repentance and remission of sin should be preached in his name among all nations, beginning at Jerusalem, I began to understand. Now I know that the blood of Jesus Christ cleanses us from all sin and that the evidence of love is not that we love him but that he loved us and gave himself as a propitiation on our behalf. Now I look forward to the day when I shall stand with that throng, a glimpse of which I was granted, and shall cry, 'Worthy art Thou to take the book, and to open the seals thereof: for Thou wast slain, and hast redeemed us to God by Thy blood out of every kindred, and tongue, and people, and nation.'"

How about you, Paul. Do you understand the cross?

"Once I did not. Once I hated the Nazarene, and I persecuted his followers for worshiping him as God because this was blasphemy. Once I stood by and watched men stone Stephen to death. Once I was crucifying the Son of God afresh. But one day I saw him: saw him in glory, saw him as he revealed himself to me with his wounds as I traveled on the road to Damascus. Now I know. I do not know him any longer after the flesh, but after the spirit. Now I am crucified with Christ, nevertheless I live; yet not I, but Christ liveth in me. Now God forbid that I should glory save in the cross of our Lord Jesus Christ. For now I know that God was in Christ, reconciling the world unto himself, and has committed unto us the gospel of reconciliation."

My friend, do you understand Calvary? Is Calvary a mystery to you? Are your eyes veiled? If you have seen him with the eyes of faith as he was crucified for you, the veil has been taken away and you understand. If not, pray at this season that you may have your eyes opened, that you may see the necessity of Calvary, that you may see what God has suffered for you, that you may understand the cross.

THE INEVITABLE CROSS

DAVID H. C. READ

A few years ago *Time* magazine printed the results of an inquiry in which thirty people were given a hundred famous events in history and asked to list them in order of importance. The result of the poll was interesting. Top place was given to Columbus's discovery of America. In the fourteenth place three events were placed equal: the discovery of X-rays, the Wright brothers' first plane flight, and the crucifixion of Jesus Christ.

Among those making this judgment there must have been members and adherents of the Christian church, that is to say, men and women who had countless times confessed their belief that the crucified and risen Christ is the Savior of the world. How did they reconcile the tremendous affirmations that they made in church with the fact that the cross of Christ shares fourteenth place in order of importance for mankind?

We have to ask, then, what we really mean when we speak of the cross. Is it a unique event which changed the course of history and can

---

David H. C. Read is a native of Scotland and has served as pastor of the Madison Avenue Presbyterian Church of New York City since 1956. He received his education from Daniel Stewart's College, Edinburgh, and the University of Edinburgh. He is an ordained minister of the Church of Scotland. He delivered the Warrick Lectures in Preaching in 1951. He served as Chaplain to the Queen in Scotland 1952–55. He is the author of *The Spirit of Life, Call It a Day, The Communication of the Gospel,* and other books as well as many periodical articles.

---

change the course of your life and mine today? Or is it an ancient symbol to which we pay respect in church but which has little place in our everyday thinking? Was Paul right when he came to Corinth declaring: "I determined not to know any thing among you, save Jesus Christ, and him crucified" (1 Corinthians 2:2)? Or was Bernard Shaw right when he dismissed what he called "Crosstianity" as a product of the diseased imagination of this same Paul?

Many of my sermons end with some kind of reference to the cross. This is not because I feel the necessity to make a final bow to orthodox doctrine no matter how far my thoughts may have ranged. It is because every preacher who derives his message from the Scriptures is magnetically drawn to this central mystery of which they speak—the death of the Son of God. And it is also because the more experience one has of life, the more we find the true answers to lie in the profundities that cannot be expressed in the logic of the mind. The Bible is entirely right when it says that the preaching of the cross, which can be offensive to the moralist, and ridiculous to the sophisticated, becomes to the believer the power and the wisdom of God.

So we begin with the cross and we stay with the cross. For the preacher it is inevitable, inescapable; and not only for the preacher. Anyone who is drawn with an open mind toward Christ will have to reckon with the fact that his life was cut short about the age of thirty by an ignominious Roman execution. For the Jewish people to whom he belonged, such a death was not only a physical but also a spiritual horror—and inconceivable for one who claimed to be God's Messiah. For the philosophers and religious teachers of the Graeco-Roman world it was an absurdity to suppose that God could reveal himself in such a sordid event. Yet the New Testament writers—in the Gospels and Epistles—not only make no attempt to hush the matter up, but also they go out of their way to describe the crucifixion in vivid detail and return to it again and again as the compulsive center of their newfound faith.

So it has been in the witness of the church from the beginning. On the day of Pentecost, Peter rose up before the crowd and said quite bluntly: "You killed him . . . but God has raised him up" (see Acts 2:23-24). From Jerusalem the story fanned out over the entire world and has spoken to the conscience of all mankind. And always there has been this note of our personal implication in this deed: "You killed him—but look what God has done and can do for you." No one can claim to be seriously concerned with Christianity and escape this inevitable cross. In every age attempts are made to bury it like the Dead Sea Scrolls in some cave and to construct a faith based simply on the teaching of Jesus. But as Paul said to King Herod Agrippa: "This thing was not done in a corner"—and the cross rears up again against the Calvary sky, inevitable, inescapable, and demanding a decision.

Authentic Christianity has always known that the cross speaks to us the unique word of Jesus Christ. It is the climax of his teaching. It is inseparable from his life. It is the point to which the whole Bible story leads and from which the Christian church starts out. No matter how attractive some diluted versions of the faith may be with their elimination of the cross and their appeal to our desire for a simple ethical code by which to live, they lack the dimension that only this word can bring.

One April afternoon many years ago I conducted a funeral service for two prisoners of war who had died of starvation and exhaustion. A thin procession, headed by an old farm cart, passed out through the gates of a camp that lay under a pall of gloom and despair—the darkest hour before the dawn of liberation. We headed slowly for a little wood a mile away. Halfway there, the little cortege broke into a trot to avoid a sudden swooping attack by six of our own planes. I spoke the words of committal to the sound of strafing just beyond the wood, and the bodies were lowered into a rough hole in the ground. Five years prisoners, living on hope, and now they lay in this deserted wood. No human words can say anything—only the words that come from the one with nail prints in his hands: "I am the resurrection and the life."

Two summers ago I stood on that same spot. The old camp is now a flourishing little town of refugees from East Germany. And when I took the road again and traced the path to the little wood, I found a most beautiful and well-tended cemetery. There the men I had buried lay with other prisoners from America, from Britain, from France, and from Russia, and with them were the new graves of German refugees. And above them all, rising on a simple arch at the entrance gate rose a large plain cross. In the sunshine of that day there fell upon the graves of so-called friend and foe, upon the memories of a common suffering and a mysterious fate, the shadow of Calvary. There is no other place to understand such things.

"Now is my soul troubled; and what shall I say? Father, save me from this hour: but for this cause came I unto this hour" (John 12:27, KJV). When we begin to understand the power of this inevitable cross to speak where men's cleverest words are "as sounding brass or a tinkling cymbal," we find new meaning in the mysterious force that seemed to impel our Lord along that Via Dolorosa. Now that it has happened, the cross is unavoidable for us. Its mark is set deep in human history, and our common life bears the scar of this divine sacrifice, this judgment, and this tremendous sympathy. But the question rises: Was it inevitable for him? Could Jesus have escaped his cross?

No one can read the last chapters of our four Gospels without a sense that events were moving with an inexorable precision to the determined end. From the moment Peter confessed him as Christ, and He set his face to go to Jerusalem, the words of Jesus were of his appointed end, and everything that happened thereafter seemed to contribute with a terrible inevitability to his fate: "The Son of man goeth as it is written of him."

What kind of inevitability is this? Is it the inevitability of what we call fate with a capital "F"? Did Jesus go to his cross because he and Pilate and Judas (and you and I) are all helpless victims of a prearranged plan—actors in a film that has already been shot, flickering across the screen to play our appointed parts?

> The Moving Finger writes; and having writ
> Moves on: nor all thy Piety nor Wit
> Shall lure it back to cancel half a Line,
> Nor all thy Tears wash out a Word of it.

The philosophy of Omar Khayyam is totally foreign to the Gospels. Read the story again and you will find that none of the men involved are considered mere victims of our inscrutable fate. Whatever mysterious words the Bible uses about the controlling pattern of our lives, it always shows us men and women as responsible agents, capable of choice; and our environment is not the steely chamber of our implacable fate, but the presence of the living God. Judas might have refused the bribe; the Sanhedrin might have decided not to condemn; Pilate may well have tossed a mental coin before he said, "Set Barabbas free." And Jesus? Was there no real conflict in his spirit, no other avenue really open to him? "Now is my soul troubled; and what shall I say? Father, save me from this hour" (John 12:27, KJV). Was that prayer a mockery—as all prayer must be if fate is in control?

It seems to me quite plain that, when he had spoken these words, he could have summoned up supernatural power to dominate the situation, as once before in his hometown, when the mob was ready to lynch him, we read that "he passing through the midst of them went away" (Luke 4:30). Isn't this what he meant when he said in Gethsemane: "Do you think that I cannot appeal to my Father, and he will at once send me more than twelve legions of angels?" (Matthew 26:53). And it seems equally plain that instead of going to Gethsemane that night he could have continued on over the Mount of Olives and taken the Galilee road which must have lain open and inviting in the light of the Passover moon.

No. There was no inevitability dictated by fate. Was it then what we call the inevitability of circumstance and human folly? There are times in history when a tragedy happens which need not have happened—except for the apparently inevitable combination of circumstances and men's mistakes. Winston Churchill has called World War II the "unnecessary war." It need not have happened. It was not decreed by fate. And yet the follies of the thirties—the blindness of the peaceful, the skill and power of the wicked, and the indifference of masses—produced together the circumstances that sparked the conflagration. Did Jesus die, then, as a result of the crimes and follies of men and nations, adding up to a situation where he was their inevitable victim?

It looks rather like it. How many on Palm Sunday in Jerusalem—if a poll had been taken—really wanted him to be crucified? Probably not more than a handful. Yet a week later it had happened. The Pharisees probably did not want such a violent course, but they were trapped in the net of their prestige. The Sadducees were not bloodthirsty scoundrels, but they had a strong political motivation to eliminate trouble with the Roman power. Pilate had no animus against Jesus whatever, but his job came first, and the reports that might be sent to Rome. These accidents combined with a sudden weakness and treachery within the group of his disciples to make the crucifixion a foregone conclusion. So this is how it happened? With this kind of inevitability?

If this were the true answer, we should expect the crucifixion to be described as a terrible accident and Jesus portrayed as a hapless victim. But there is not a line of this kind in the record. Jesus moved through the network of crime and circumstance with the sure step of one who knew what he was doing and what would be done to him.

The agony of decision was not the less real. "Now is my soul troubled; and what shall I say?" (John 12:27, KJV). This is not an inhuman demigod for whom pain, loneliness, and the brutal curtain of death mean nothing. He shares with us the shrinking and the agony. Yet through the tumult of his soul and the dark temptations that flooded back with the demons of the wilderness inviting him to take another way, there sounded the calm strong voice of ultimate decision. "Now is my soul troubled; and what shall I say? Father, save me from this hour: but for this cause came I unto this hour" (John 12:27, KJV).

"For this cause." With these words his destiny is clear. He came to die. The cross which was now almost within sight would be freely chosen. Why? Because there was no other way in which he could reach to the depth of the human agony he came to share, to "bear our griefs and carry our sorrows." And because there was no other way in which he could draw upon himself the hopeless weight of our sins and expose and absorb the evil that blocks us from the holiness of God. "The Lord hath laid on him the iniquity of us all" (Isaiah 53:6, KJV). The only way a God of perfect peace and joy can reach his suffering family is in this amazing way to share that suffering. The only way a God of perfect purity and goodness can reach his disobedient people is to offer himself as the sacrifice for sin. What we see in the cross is not the hideous outworking of blind fatality nor a tragic accident of history. We see the end result of God's redeeming love going out to seek us where we are. "For this cause came I into the world." The inevitability is the inevitability of love.

This is why the story of the cross is the greatest story in the world and why, whenever we hear it, we face a life-or-death decision. For the Christ who died brings us right up against the ultimate choice. Faced with this demonstration of God's love, do I continue to grasp my life for myself or do I yield myself to him who loved me and gave himself for me, and so go on to live?

BACKWARDS OR FORWARDS?

SAMUEL M. SHOEMAKER

The Sunday after Easter is often called "Low Sunday" for obvious reasons. The crowd is not here that was here last Sunday. Even we ourselves feel a little letdown. We have come through the long season of Lent; we have lived through the critical days of Jerusalem with our Lord; we have seen the crowds welcome him and then the leaders crucify him with the mob calling for his blood. And then comes the great climax of Easter. It is always for us a day of supreme power and joy. But there is something about all that buildup and climax that takes it out of you just a little.

What do we do after such a great elation? When there has come into our lives a great emotional or spiritual climax, what happens next?

I think there are two different things which we may do. One is that increasingly we begin to distrust the elation and call it pure emotion. We turn back to life's less colorful but familiar routines, and we say to ourselves that these responsibilities constitute the only real

---

Samuel M. Shoemaker received his education from Princeton University, General Seminary, and Union Seminary of New York. From 1917 to 1924 he served as YMCA secretary. He became Rector of Calvary Church, New York, in 1925. In 1952 he became Rector of Calvary Church, Pittsburgh. He was a founder of Alcoholics Anonymous and the Pittsburgh Experiment of Faith at Work. More than two dozen books poured from his able pen, including *The Experiment of Faith* and *Beginning Your Ministry,* as well as many articles and pamphlets.

---

living. Some of us pride ourselves upon our unemotional natures, look with disdain upon those who allow themselves to thrill very much, and feel more at home among those concerns of life which do not take so much emotion but rather the dogged pursuit of the customary. After all, the pitch of emotion is hard to hold, while the daily drive of duty is within every man's grasp. We often cheat ourselves out of great new heights of living, out of great fresh insights into the meaning of our existence, by saying things like this to ourselves.

And the other course is to recognize the reality of what has taken place, and to envision life afresh in the light of it. To be sure, we must return to life's routines and responsibilities, but they ought to shine with a new meaning. We ought to see in the daily chores new possibilities, new vistas of accomplishment and reward. The elation and emotion of the great moment that lies behind us ought to trickle down into the dryness and customariness of our routine and moisten it as rain does dry ground. There should be new energy in the moment of insight and elation that will transform what we have to do in the daily grind and make it infinitely more than it used to be.

Simon Peter is always a help to us, and he is a help here. He was of a profoundly emotional nature. He responded to human needs and to divine calls. He gave himself with abandon and enthusiasm. We may be sure that as the iron of Good Friday entered into his soul, with the memory of his denial and disloyalty, so the resurrection was for him an immensely emotional experience. To make up your mind for almost forty-eight hours that your beloved Master was dead, to know you had failed him in the crisis, and then suddenly to discover that he was alive again so you could go and tell him how sorry you were, and begin with him again—this was a profoundly shaking experience. Some time after the resurrection, Peter was back again in Galilee. I wonder why he went. Our Lord had promised to meet him in Galilee; possibly that is why he went. But there may have been another reason. Did Simon Peter want to go back among the familiar scenes where he had lived and worked formerly and test himself out on all this Christian discipleship? Did he want to see how he really felt about this overwhelming contrast between Good Friday and Easter, and what was his considered judgment about the resurrection when you put it all up against the simple life of catching fish? I do not know. When we meet him in the last chapter of John, he is with some of his friends by the old familiar lakeside in Galilee, saying to them, "I go a fishing."

What did that mean to him? Was it the first step in a possible reversion to the old life—the old safe life of the fishing business? It may have been only temporary enjoyment of his well-loved art and trade; but I am inclined to think there was just a little temptation for him in this. I think it stood for the old pre-Christian days when life had asked relatively little of him, when he had been just a decent, honest, self-respecting, wife-supporting fisherman up there by the lake of Galilee. It had all been very different from following a Man whose very name caused controversy, a Man who made stupendous claims and then backed them up, who asked tremendous sacrifices and expected them, who stirred things up and was uncontent to let well enough alone. His had been a very stormy career. It ended with a violent death. And then there was that great mystery of the resurrection. They had seen him, to be sure, but the point was, which life should Simon Peter choose once and for all—the life he knew and understood, the life where he was sure he was headed for a decent income and a happy old age in the village or the life he only partially understood, the life where he was headed for he did not know what, probably martyrdom like his Master's? After all, he must have said to himself, you can't always live on the mountaintop excitement of these days since the resurrection. Wouldn't it be better to write the thing off as too emotional, as too impossible ever really to reach, and just go back to this which I know and can do? I strongly suspect that as he saw a fish darting through the water and flung over it his net with its little weights at the corners to pin the fish down on the bottom, some very long thoughts were going through his mind. Which life, which loyalties, which values? Was it to be everything that net stood for, or was he verily to catch men as Jesus had long ago told him he would do?

That struggle is not confined to Simon Peter on the shore of Galilee long ago; that struggle meets everyone of us again and again through our lives.

An alteration in circumstances can be the occasion of going forward, or of continuing with our customary way which is often almost the same thing as going backwards. A new position carries us to another city. The loss of someone in the family alters the home situation and asks different responsibilities of us. We make a new departure in our lives, and it calls on new muscles of the mind, new effort, new imagination. Shall all this be a step up, or a step down? I don't mean in the eyes of the world, nor in any worldly way, but in character and in faith and in the quality of human relations. It all depends, I think, upon whether we have prayed about this change and made it in the belief that God wants us to make it. It depends on whether we take God with us more fully than ever before into the new circumstances. It depends upon whether we let him control the flow of new emotions which the altered circumstances arouse in us. A departure in life seems to me more than a change in outward circumstance. I wonder if God does not mean it to be a whole new vision of life itself, and what God wants life to be, and what he expects us to make of it. A change may be a demotion in the eyes of the world but a promotion from God's angle if it makes us face the real things more honestly. I have seen ministers take smaller parishes than they had to the infinite benefit of their own souls, and therefore of their people's. But the point is, these changes are a kind of plowing of the spirit: shall the next crop be richer or shall it be more full of weeds? Is it to be forwards, or backwards?

But it is especially in connection with some exalted spiritual experience that I want to consider this truth. We all know that if we seek, we find. My friend Rufus Moseley once said to me, "If you seek Jesus as you think he is, he will reveal himself to you as he really is." Now somewhere in our spiritual pilgrimage, God will reach in with a luminous thought, or a lifting sense that we are not pursuing a chimera but the veriest reality in the universe. On our knees, or as we talk in prayer, or as we talk with another who is spiritually illuminated, something will "come" to us that turns on the light. We ought to put down such things in a spiritual notebook, for they are easy to forget, and may be meant for milestones in our spiritual journey. I saw a fine booklet that was just the compilation of one man's discoveries of this nature. Shall these things be just "ideas," or shall the "word be made flesh" so that they become part of our living? Fewer words more richly appropriated would mean a richer spiritual existence for most of us.

Or we come to a service like we had last Sunday morning. Through the music and flowers and the glorious sense of our Lord's victory there is given us a vision of what our life ought to be. This glory of his was not easily attained. As the beautiful collect says, he "entered not into glory before he was crucified." We know that if we pursued this vision steadily, it would cut out of our life not all pleasure but all frivolity and wrong and dividedness of mind between Christ and the world. Which way do we go—backwards, or forwards?—backwards towards the familiar version of "I go a fishing," or forwards toward the unknown with Christ which was the way Simon Peter finally went? Many said positive words to me after the service last Sunday. Are they here today? Are they going to be here right along? Was this emotion, or was it reality? It all depends on what they do with the experience. It rests between themselves and God.

And sometimes God reaches right into the life of a man or a woman. I saw him do it not long ago. At a stroke, he lifted someone to a whole new level of living. What is that man going to do; is he going to make all the old habits subservient to this new gift of life that God has given him, or is he going to try to mix them and compromise, or is he frankly going back to the old level to look back one day on this as a chimerical, transient, emotional experience? Is he going to make all his professional practice conform to this new experience, let it pervade every relationship, cut compromise and halfway measures, or drag this new experience down into the old ways? For Simon Peter, this old fishing business was just a temporary return to the familiar, unless he was going back on Christ altogether. But there is business in the world to be done. Some men have got to stay by. They must both catch fish and catch men. Most people in the church behave entirely too much like everybody round about them when it comes to everyday living. Instead of lifting home life and business life to the level of Christian conversion, they compromise Christian conversion with the world. You know when you hear them say, "I go a fishing," that the higher level is a thing of the past. Is it with you? Did Easter show you something about yourself and your daily occupation that you had not seen before? Have you already forgotten it, let it grow dim, or did you let God take hold of you and begin a new life within you?

Let us pray that in the moment when we say, "I go a fishing," and turn backwards to the old familiar things, Christ may come to us as he came to Simon Peter that morning on the beach of Galilee and remind us that with him we can never go backwards, but only forwards.

THE HURTING AND HEALING GAZE OF GOD

K. M. SWENSON

After I had reprimanded my young son for riding his wagon in the garden, crushing my marigolds, he looked into my stern eyes, and, filled with shame, shouted: "Don't look at me! You can't look at me!"

I realized in his reply that there was agony in his heart; there was shame that could not tolerate my gaze; there was remorse that did not want to be reminded that he had disobeyed my command not to play in the garden. His words, "Don't look at me!" had a transforming power upon me. Oh, I still looked at him, but now the severeness in my eyes changed to compassion and understanding. He had disobeyed; he had disappointed me; more than that, he was disappointed in himself and now was suffering pain in being confronted by one he loved.

It is so reminiscent of an episode in the life of Christ's disciple, Peter. All the disciples were in the upper room, celebrating that Passover—what we know now as the Last Supper. Jesus suggested that, before the night was over, all his disciples would desert him. Peter, with all intentions of being a faithful disciple, replied that, even

K. M. Swenson, a native of Kansas, received his education from Pacific Lutheran University, Tacoma, Washington, and the Lutheran School of Theology, Chicago, Illinois. Ordained in 1968 by the Lutheran Church of America, Mr. Swenson has pastored churches in Great Falls, Montana, and Seattle, Washington, and is now pastor of Faith Lutheran Church, Bellingham, Washington. He is married and the father of three children.

though the rest should run away, he would not. But Jesus, because he knew so well how men act in great temptation, responded to him by saying that, before the night was past, Peter would deny him three times.

You know the story. Jesus was arrested, and the disciples fled. But Peter, when he came to his senses, returned to the scene of Jesus' trial. Then the test took place. He was accused of being mixed up with the prisoner. Loyalty took a back seat, and Peter denied that he even knew Jesus.

As we read on, Jesus turned and looked at Peter. Oh, the pain he must have felt as he saw the dejected eyes of the Master come his way. How crushing it is to be caught in the act, to be reminded that we are not faithful, to have our disobedience underscored by eyes that have seen and know! We read that Peter wept bitterly; we can imagine him covering his face, sobbing: "Don't look at me!"

Peter hated to have Jesus look at him, but, at the look of Jesus, Peter recognized his own sin; and how depressing that is! Next to the shame of public opinion, nothing is more difficult to overcome than the pinpricks of the conscience.

As I looked at my marigolds and then at my son, I thought of Jesus when he looked at Peter. Here was a man who had just betrayed his Lord; in so doing, he had also betrayed himself. Yet, within Jesus' look, there was not bitterness and hatred, as we might expect. In character with this whole ministry and his attitude toward men, there must have been within those eyes the look of understanding and forgiveness.

This is consistently the picture we have of Christ as he portrayed what God is like. This is just one more example of the way in which God accepts each one of us, despite the severity of our faults, despite the damaging lack of control that we demonstrate constantly. This points up so beautifully the divine economy, as God sends his Son to obtain for us the salvation that we are too weak to earn for ourselves.

Yet, we constantly try to escape the eyes of God, who might find us out. As we repeatedly run headlong into gardens and over marigolds, into demoralizing dilemmas and over the lives of many who are victims of our lack of concern or of our aggressions, how we dread the thought of an all-knowing God and the omnipresent eyes which note the fall of a sparrow and the disobedience of men. "Don't look at me!" becomes the repeated refrain of guilt-ridden man.

The picture in Genesis has Adam and Eve hiding in the garden after their traitorous and rebellious deed, in the hope that they could escape the reprimanding eyes of God: "The man and his wife heard the sound of the Lord God walking in the garden at the time of the evening breeze and hid from the Lord God among the trees of the garden. But the Lord God called out to the man and said to him, 'Where are you?'" (Genesis 3:8-9, NEB).

That is the way it always is. We want to cry out, "Don't look at me," but God is always asking, "Where are you?" You see, the creator God cannot tolerate a relationship that has broken and is deteriorating. We want to hide the loose ends, but God is continually trying to splice them.

Our efforts are consistently to hide our face from God, but he is seeking to find us. It's strange, the methods he uses. We think we have outgrown the guiding hand of God; then we are faced with a situation far beyond our strength or ability to handle. We think we can find fulfillment and peace of mind through material goods, but we find our desires too bottomless to fill, or we are bored, or we are anxious. We think we have failed too completely to warrant the presence of God, but we feel his comfort. In our own defense we want to yell, "Don't look at me!" but we rejoice at the answer, "Where are you?" Oh, the joy when we think we are lost and God declares that we are found!

It is a tragedy that, while we try in every way and wish with all our wishes that God will not see us in our guilt and shame, it is only the compassionate and forgiving eye of God that can soothe our guilt and heal our shame. The Bible is full of such phrases as, "He looked on them and had compassion." We are consistently reminded that the pure eyes of God always point out our weaknesses in contrast; yet the glance of those eyes is necessary for us to feel forgiven and freed of exactly what we hate being.

In the case of Adam and Eve, it was only as God looked upon the sins of floundering man that we received the guidance of the prophets and ultimately the salvation of the Christ. God saw where we were and declared to us that, through his forgiveness, we were pure and could once again tolerate his gaze.

In the case of Peter, it was only after God had looked at Peter, bringing to a head Peter's feelings of remorse and assuring him of his love, that Peter surged to become a leader of God's church and was enabled to respond to Christ's departing words: "Peter, follow me . . . feed my lambs" (see John 21:22, 16, NEB).

And it was Jesus on the cross who, as he looked at one and then another of his betrayers, said: "Father, forgive them; for they know not what they do" (Luke 23:34).

This is the result of the look of Christ upon us. His eyes are forgiving, even though we falter and fall because we do not see the dismaying consequences of what we are doing. His look is compassionate and takes into account the temptations of the season, understands our guilt, and restores to us the joy of one who is pure.

How hopeless our lives would be if we were forever to hide our faces from God's gaze, if we were not to pray that God would look upon our situation with the fullness of his love and acceptance, or if we were not anxious to look back into his eyes with a prayer of thanksgiving for having been found!

If we are not conscious of the eyes of God, we may never feel the compulsion to ask forgiveness.

If God does not look we may never know the compassion and acceptance with which he deals with us.

If we do not look back into the eyes of God, we may never know the assurance that he keeps on looking and caring and loving.

THE PARADOX OF THE CROSS

RODRIGO D. TANO

In First Corinthians Paul puts in sharp contrast the world's value system and God's way of viewing things (1 Corinthians 1:18-31).

The world considers the message about a crucified Savior absurd and revolting. God regards the value system of the world as distorted and foolish.

There is more than contrast in the text; there is paradox: foolish things shaming the wise, weak things shaming the strong, nonentities nullifying things which are. When God, the Infinite One, assumed creaturely existence and expressed his thoughts in earthly categories, there was both mystery and paradox.

What psychological reversal could have changed the disgrace and defeat of Golgotha into triumph and glory? How could the "foolish" message of a crucified Savior be a sign of wisdom? How could a defenseless and defeated Man be considered mighty to save? This is the paradox of the cross.

A native of the Philippines, **Rodrigo D. Tano** began his ministry as a preacher of the gospel in 1952 under the influence of the Christian and Missionary Alliance church. Later Mr. Tano joined the faculty of the Christian and Missionary Alliance Bible College in Zamboanga City and afterward was named president. Recently he was released from his position to pursue further studies in the United States. He is currently enrolled in a doctoral program at Baylor University, Waco, Texas.

The cross was a horrible instrument of death. It was fit only for condemned slaves and the most despised criminals. Cicero described the repulsiveness of the cross to the Romans in these words: "Let the very name of the cross be far away not only from the body of a Roman citizen, but even from his thoughts, his eyes, his ears."

Similarly the Jews detested the cross, for it was written in their law that a "hanged man is accursed by God" (Deuteronomy 21:23; cf. Galatians 3:13). The message about a crucified Messiah was to the Jews a disappointment, a crushing of their hope for an all-conquering political champion.

The Greek ideal was a harmonious, rational, and beautiful universe. To the Greek mind also the cross and its message was ugly, tragic, and foolish, stultifying to the intellect. In more modern days Friedrich Nietzsche and Bertrand Russell rejected Christianity because of its insistence on humility and self-denial. They affirmed that belief in God is not for the tough-minded.

How then can so "foolish" a scheme as the cross be the mark of divine wisdom? How can a man of integrity and intelligence believe in the incredible and absurd?

Paul's answer is a categorical assertion that those who reject the message of the cross are on the way to destruction. He says that God has decreed to destroy all human schemes of salvation, no matter how brilliant they may be, and to thwart the "cleverness of the clever." The best that the Egyptians could do was to deify the sacred bull. The Romans set up their emperor as a god and the Phoenicians created a fish-man diety. The Greeks glorified the human intellect.

"Where is the wise man? Where is the scribe? Where is the debater of this age? Has not God made foolish the wisdom of the world?" The world cannot know God in a redemptive sense by its own striving. There is a sense in which philosophy may be compared to a "blind man, in a dark room, looking for a black cat that is not there."

The futility of man's speculative quest for the ultimate origin, nature, and purpose of all things is expressed by William James in a note found on his desk after his death: "There is no conclusion. What has been concluded that we might conclude in regard to it? There are no fortunes to be told and there is no advice to be given. Farewell."

Even so, God has arranged it this way, so that the world may find God only through the divinely appointed means: the message of the cross. Wisdom is the best use of the best means to attain the ends desired. It is in this sense that the cross upon which Christ died is the mark of God's wisdom. Through it salvation has been accomplished.

The second part of the paradox of the cross is that divine weakness is strength. Admittedly, Christ was weak and powerless when he hung on the cross. When the mob demanded that he come down from the cross to prove his Messiahship, he refused to do so. How can a weak and defeated Messiah be the mighty Savior?

Power is not merely the display of physical strength. Rather, it is the achievement of purpose. The purpose of the cross has been achieved, as millions around the world can testify. By the cross the whole cosmic order has been reconciled to God and will ultimately be retrieved from moral and physical corruption.

While philosophers like Plato, Aristotle, and the Stoics have advanced some of man's highest ethical ideals, they have failed to provide the enabling power to achieve those ideals. Where human wisdom and power end, Christianity comes in to offer the highest ideal and provide the means of attaining it. Indeed, the "foolishness of God is wiser than men, and the weakness of God is stronger than men."

In his own inimitable way God allowed the tragedy of Calvary in order to show his wisdom, to reverse the world's value system, and to enable men to boast not in themselves but in God alone. This is why the crucified Messiah is all in all to those who believe: wisdom, righteousness, holiness, and redemption. What a grand design!

The principle of the cross condemns all reliance on human ingenuity and power to accomplish the plans and purposes of God. It lays aside all schemes of salvation which are separated from Christ. The apostle Paul determined to preach the gospel, but "not with eloquent wisdom, lest the cross of Christ be emptied of its power" (1 Corinthians 1:17). He refused to boast "except in the cross of our Lord Jesus Christ" (Galatians 6:14). Horatius Bonar wrote:

> The cross it standeth fast.
> Hallelujah! Hallelujah!
> Defying every blast,
> Hallelujah! Hallelujah!
> The winds of hell have blown,
> The world its hate hath shown,
> Yet it is not overthrown,
> Hallelujah for the cross!